The Christmas Epistles

AN ADVENT OF INCARNATION

JACK GROBLEWSKI

DREAM
TREE
PRESS

Illustrations by Vince Steckle

Cover Design by Kendall Nicole Studios, kendallnicolestudios.com

Dream Tree Press, 8627 Bernard Rd. Sanger, Texas 76266
dreamtreepress@gmail.com

These reflections are dedicated to my wife Trish and to all of those both near and far who have harangued me over the years to put these words to print.

Contents

Foreword

BY STUART BELL

FOR MANY YEARS, IRENE AND I have been urging our good friend Jack to publish his writings. Our prayers have finally been answered! Through the years, we have read most of Jack's Christmas letters. It would be true to say that the opening of our Christmas mail and finding an envelope stamped in the USA would fill our hearts with genuine joy and anticipation. Definitely a highlight of the Christmas season, we always wondered what new angle Jack would bring to the gospel narrative. We love the magic and mystery of Christmas and our house has been highly influenced by Bethlehem Pennsylvania, as each window displays a Moravian candle, not just during Advent but all through the year.

This is a special book for a number of reasons. Firstly, it contains musings, prayers and writings of over thirty years of authentic ministry. Also, it is an interesting blend of the prophetic, the poetic, the theological and the pastoral all in one volume. This is not designed for a fast read, and would perhaps be best approached like a spiritual meal, one bite at a time, over the days of Advent, making way for a Christ-focused Christmas. It is the kind of book that can be read over and over again, bringing fresh light and illumination to the Incarnation. These letters are well-worth pondering.

I remember as a boy being stirred by a classic Charles Wesley hymn speaking of the incredible truth of the Incarnation: 'God contracted to a span, incomprehensibly made man.' Few of us could summarise such majestic thoughts in so few words. However, Jack Groblewski's gifted writing makes these complex mysteries accessible to the searching mind. Presented in this book is a creative collection of Advent thoughts and contemplations, penned in the form of Christmas letters that have been gathered over a number of decades.

Through each year's letter, the Christmas story comes to life. The ancient prophecies; the angel visits; the backdrop of a cruel and oppressive world; the Magi guided by starlight; shepherds woken and stunned by angel choirs and a young Jewish virgin girl giving birth to the Son of God.

Jack digs deeply into scripture and with God-given imagination, vividly paints with words the wonderful story of the birth of Jesus: the saviour of the world, the one born to be king.

May you experience, as we have, the wonder of it all this Christmas.

-*Stuart Bell, Alive Church, Lincoln, England*

Preface

HOW TO USE THIS DEVOTIONAL BOOK

THE NOTION OF GOD BECOME MAN has both perplexed and charmed me from my earliest memories of my grandmother, a devout and bullish Polish Catholic, dragging my younger brother and I to a small chapel at Christmas time. She and my great aunt, adorned in their babushkas and unable to carry us, would nevertheless forcibly convey us to the front where a nativity with marble figures awaited. They would then direct us to kiss the marble baby in the manger. And she would say, *"bojie."* a diminutive of the word for Lord or God in Polish. It was about as close to a catechism as my grandmother could create!

The marble our lips touched was ice cold, but I remember a certain warmth at the notion. It was not quite a Wesleyan "heart strangely warmed" moment, but something vaguely spiritual was still happening in me. Years later as a young adult, when I committed my heart to Christ, I found myself captured by the thought of an all-powerful, omnipotent, omnipresent God become an infant child. The preponderance of the mystery was overwhelming: the fullness of God in so slight a being! It made me think of George MacDonald's poem:

Where did you come from baby dear?
From out of everywhere and into here.

This is an Advent devotional, but it is not a typical representation of the genre. It is designed to invite you into the mystery of incarnation and join us in being captured by the wonder of God become man. Let me first, however, invite you into the origin story of this particular collection of writing.

One is tempted these days to identify the time leading up to Christmas as a secular holiday season that parallels the Christmas observance. But the roots of the secular season are embedded in the theological and historical Christmas and Advent, often to the chagrin of those who work hard to camouflage that fact in some way. Most of the themes that see displayed in the culture find their moorings in celebrations of the first nativity. Family gathering, traveling from afar, gift giving, peace on earth, celebrations of lights and stars, gatherings for the poor, the destitute and the refugees are just a few of the themes that pour forth from the scripture narratives. So, there is a constant interplay, sometimes, tense, between the secular and the sacred at this time of year. Tim Keller in his book *Hidden Christmas,* says it well when he describes a Christian carol playing in a department store as a sacred "uninvited visitor" to the secular season.

On the other hand, we have the modern Sauls of Tarsus who compulsively feel the need to defend the sanctity of Christmas by assaulting the froth and bubble of secular commercialism by breathing subliminal threats at the advertisements and displays from their pulpits. Or they create slogans and bumper stickers to irritate their 'ignorant' neighbors who really are just looking to get in on the fun. "He is the reason for the season," they declare--as if the real Christmas can no longer defend itself in the face of what they see as exploitation!

That is not to say that the commercialization of Christmas has not cost the church. With the church leaning into more secular modes of expression to accommodate the perceived needs of congregations, times of preparation and any pauses dedicated to reflection have lapsed along with the liturgies. Seasonal fatigue is a complaint commonly heard in churches during the weeks preceding Christmas! How will we all actually "fit in" all of the expectations amassed over the course of the year? The office parties, the gift buying, and the family's expectations are all well-fueled by the advertising industry. Chevy Chase's caricature in *National Lampoon's Christmas Vacation* mirrors our approach toward Christmas, so that it seems there is a little bit of Clark Griswold in each of us! (Interestingly, it is a film that has only one overt allusion to God.) My theory is that Christmas devotionals are currently proliferating because so many are looking for a way to break this spell of commercialization.

Years ago, as a young pastor, when I noticed that the observance of Christmas and Advent was trending in my congregation as outward busy-ness that marginalized reflection on the mystery, I chose to forego Christmas cards and instead send devotional letters, or rather "prose poems". The amount of response I received was startling. After retiring from the senior position in the church, I have been encouraged to gather the letters into this book of Christmas Epistles, which I deeply encourage you to use. These letters are personal and, to be honest, somewhat dense. They are actual letters sent to hundreds of people around the world and they are poetic for a purpose.

This is my addition to the Christmas devotional bookshelf with a bit of a different spin. The goal of this devotional is to create a gravitas of soul concerning the truth of the Incarnation itself and then to generate a new vitalized intimacy with the One who is the Incarnation Himself. The book is in three parts: this Preface and an Introduction, the Advent devotional itself, and then a short essay on the mystery of the Incarnation. There are twenty-five devotionals. Each devotional is followed by a prayer.

The most comprehensive way to approach the book is to read the thumbnail history of Christmas, which is an easy, short passage. Then to read the essay on the Incarnation, which is a less simple and longer piece. Then, approach each devotional on each day of Advent moving into Christmas. Please remember again that the "epistles" were produced over twenty-five years. Read the letter in the morning as if my wife Trish and I are sending it to you personally. If you are reading it, we have prayed for you. Pray the prayer on the following page of each letter and let the theme dwell in you throughout the day. Ask yourself and God questions regarding the theme and the wish for the season. If you have a prayer partner or a spouse, discuss it. Pray about it and through it. Let each letter inhabit each day until the day of His advent.

Alternatively, anyone can forego these suggestions and "cherry pick" the calendar as it suits you. You will find each letter is quite full and packed with layers of meaning and the thoughts are dense enough that the devotional can be used year after year.

Our prayer is that this is useful to prepare yourselves for Christmas.

Jack Groblewski, Bethlehem, Pennsylvania 2023

Introduction

A THUMBNAIL HISTORY OF CHRISTMAS

... Et incarnatus est de Spiritu Sancto Ex Maria Virgine,
et homo factus est.

... and by the Holy Spirit was incarnate of the Virgin Mary,
and became man.
- Nicene Creed

Christmas

No religious holiday, Christian or otherwise, connects with the
world as comprehensively and curiously as Christmas. Easter
season, to be sure, is more essential to the church, for without the
critical holy day cluster of crucifixion, resurrection, ascension and
Pentecost together, who we are as church ceases to be. This is true
irrespective of denomination or affiliation: Easter time is personal
as well as existential. Christmas, however, strikes a chord that
resonates in the secular universe in ways that the passion cannot.
The reason for the differences in the way the world reacts to
Christmas and Easter are unsurprising and yet enlightening.

The journey of Jesus from Palm Sunday to the sending of the
promised Holy Spirit on Pentecost is integrally tied to the Jewish

Calendar. Christmas is not. In fact, it is not tied to any historical calendar. No one can conclusively make the case that Jesus the Christ was born on December 25 and scholars don't try. It is true that the Eastern Orthodox and a few others identify a different date for Jesus' birth, a few weeks later, based upon a different calendar. But it is hardly something seen as crucial. And the roughly, somewhat arbitrary fixed date of December 25 does not detract from the attractiveness of the holiday and its season.

Now for some, for example Orthodox Jews living in the West, the popularity of the holiday poses some awkwardness. Yet for the less orthodox, there are plentiful contrivances to allow them to get in on the fun, including the emphasis on Hanukkah lights and bushes and playful dreidels. Where we live, in the Hindu community, the houses sport colored lights which are always a facet of Hindu celebration. And the Islamic Quranic view, though failing to honor Jesus as God nor God/man, still holds that the birth of Jesus is miraculous and virginal. Kwanzaa was fashioned in 1966 but its particular positioning on December 26th bespeaks an intention to attach it to a season of faith. These distinctions reveal a cultural response to Christmas in ways that other holidays do not inspire. Christmas has created a season of faiths broader than itself.

One touchstone of the draw of Christmas across cultures may be that it is entrenched in a universally celebrated human experience: the joy of a birth. Each of the Lenten holidays, while addressing the heart of the human condition, are not universal human experiences. Each of us has been born, but most of us have not been crucified nor even physically persecuted for what we believe. None of us has been resurrected yet. But we know what it means experientially to celebrate pregnancy and birth. And if the birth is miraculous and history changing in its impact, an extra element of transcendence is added to the joy. The Christmas story is, at the same time, full of the stuff of life but also full of the supernatural, full of the intrigue and drama surrounding the threat to what is innocent.

Christmas, in its universality, does not need a calendar date in the way that other holidays do. Most of us tend to forget that times and seasons and calendars are actually a function of physical movement. The earth rotates and hours are fixed. The moon revolves and months are defined. The earth revolves and the years are marked. To secure a date and time is to note that the universe was in a defined position that it will never be in again in quite the same way. Jesus' death on the cross aligned perfectly to the sacrifice of the Passover Lamb such that the crucifixion completed all that the Passover portended. Jesus said consummately, "It is finished." The laws of thermodynamics declare that the arrow of time moves forward and never backward, and we know that the cosmos was in a fixed position to which it shall never return when He died for us. But, the redemptive effect of His death extends forward and backward from beginning to end.

Upon Gabriel's annunciation of God's plan for her, Mary said, "Be it done unto me." And what was done was the Incarnation: God became one of us. And it is never finished, nor will it be. Jesus, both God and man, was conceived and born. Orthodox Christian doctrine insists that He is resurrected and seated at the right hand of the Father, incarnate. He became incarnate God and Man and He is yet God and man. And what is wonderful about a life that is never finished is this: He can keep on having birthdays!

And what is wonderful about a life that is never finished is this: He can keep on having birthdays!

Mark's gospel, which is probably the earliest written gospel, contains no nativity story, making Luke and Matthew the basis for all our biblical nativity stories (since John's gospel gives us an entirely different lens on Jesus' entry to earth). And while scholars have combed through these two biblical accounts for hints of specifics, neither evangelist seems terribly concerned with citing a date. Luke, who usually pays attention to timing, does offer this context. Joseph's journey from Nazareth to Bethlehem was occasioned by a census requiring him to register himself at his ancestral home, Bethlehem in Judea. And while there was a recorded census taken around the year 6CE, the homicidal, jealous king Herod would already have been dead, and it was Herod's sinister conversation with the Magi that ignited the darkest moment of the Christmas story, the slaughtering of the first-born males in Bethlehem.

So many astronomical forays into the past have attempted to come to some tacit conclusion about the migrating star that gripped the hearts of the Magi and sent them down their epic journey to find the Messiah prince. Astronomical confluences, comets and supernovas and the like have been traced by reversing astronomical models back into history. And while some of the hypotheses have proven intriguing, and the reports of the search are entertaining, the mysterious moving star yet remains a mystery for the most part. Even the wondrous star fixes no sure date.

The more surprising gospel with regards to the nativity is easily that of John. Ancient traditions with some historical support place John at the city of Ephesus for the writing of his gospel. Parallel traditions place Mary the mother of Jesus there with him. In the Western church Mary was thought to have been "assumed" into heaven from Ephesus and the Roman Catholic church celebrates the feast of that "Assumption" on August 15. The Eastern church observes a bit of a different theological spin on Mary's body being moved to heaven by celebrating "Dormition," or falling asleep, on the same date. Nevertheless, both traditions locate Mary in Ephesus with John, a positioning which would fulfill Jesus' request while He was being crucified that she would become mother to John and John a son to her. (John 19: 25-27)

Should these traditions be true (or even if they are not completely true), what is fascinating is that John, whose gospel is both later than the others and contains information that the others do not, never elaborates on the nativity narratives of Matthew and Luke. Since presumably no one had the perspective of Mary regarding these events better than John himself, his silence creates an implicit statement. Either Mary and John saw the other accounts as complete and judged them as not to be tampered with, or there was perhaps a conscious decision to transcend the infancy narratives with a sublime theology of the Word of God and the mystery of the Incarnation. In that sense one could say that the first chapter of the Gospel of John is the loftiest story of the Nativity: "And the Word became flesh and dwelt among us." (John 1:1-18)

As early as the second century, the church father Clement of Alexandria, mentions that there was interest in Egypt in dating the birth of Christ, so that it could be acknowledged or celebrated. Various dates were hypothesized by various teachers. Since Luke's shepherds were guarding their flocks by night, some inferred that the spring lambing season when sheep were guarded overnight to protect against predation and theft was the most probable timing. This occurs in early May, and it is the slight piece of evidence we gain from the shepherd's story.

Saint Augustine of Hippo does note a few centuries later that the Donatists (considered to be a heterodox sect) were in fact celebrating Christmas on December 25th. In sermon 202, *On the Trinity*, Augustine recounts a calculation that placed Jesus' conception on March 25 leading to His birth on December 25th, citing the authority of a "tradition." There were then two holy days to consider: the day of the Annunciation and the day of the Birth. Pope Julius I settled the issue in the west shortly thereafter and declared December 25th the date of the Christmas celebration which meant that the annunciation would be marked to March 25, a practice still accepted today in most of the church. The coming of the Magi or Epiphany was then celebrated on January 6, and the twelve days in between give us the twelve days of Christmas and the partridge in a pear tree. Everything finally became chronologically tidy.

Interestingly, the long-standing popular thinking has been that Christmas situates itself near the winter solstice because of a cavalcade of various pagan traditions celebrating the solstice. The celebration of the darkest day of the year finishing and the sun marching by increments toward the brightest day of the year might seem like a likely candidate for a holiday centering on hope for the world, but there is no mention of Christmas supplanting a pagan holiday in the ancient church. Much later, however, we do have the additions of European pagan traditions of Christmas trees, wreaths, logs, holly berries and the Christmas goose, all of which served to bring a northern hemispheric charm to the whole holiday enterprise.

This thumbnail sketch of the attempts at dating the holiday suggests two vital notions. The first is that the feast which marks the Incarnation and birth of Christ is so much grander than a date! The lack of a provable, fixed date has not in two thousand years diminished or dampened for a moment an appetite for the holiday itself. It is not that the fixing of the date doesn't matter: it is just that it doesn't matter much! What does matter is the heartfelt observance of the familial and spiritual feast of Christmas.

Secondly, the thousands of years described here suggest how much humanity yearns to celebrate the conception and birth of God come among us, not only physically in body and soul, but also spiritually. A hunger inside makes us want to reach into the mystery and partake! We seek to understand that which cannot be completely understood: the story of His becoming. As we reflect, our hearts become lost in the intricacies of the unfathomable process and realize that there is so much more than we knew in the saga of an age's long hope finally realized.

Yet the grandness of the Christmas season also contributes to a striking psychological and sociological contrast. People encased in memories of painful seasons past become depressed as they grapple with grief over lost family members, broken relationships, regrets, and even suicidal thinking. And situational considerations such as financial stress, feelings of isolation, or the increased pressure to socialize can layer on top of these deep issues. The professional counseling literature is replete with studies demonstrating spikes in stress levels during the holiday season. It is easy to understand the Peanuts cartoon reflection: Charlie Brown says to Linus, "I think there must be something wrong with me, Linus. Christmas is coming, but I'm not happy. I don't feel the way I'm supposed to feel."

The paradox of experiencing Christmas, then, is the immersive mystery coinciding with the demands of a holiday to be contended with. On one hand we have the theological gravitas of the Incarnation, while the other hand is heavy with the practiced annual regalia of the season. And we have the inevitable sense that we are responsible to respond to the holiday with true joy when joy is not our experienced truth. It is a devilish set up for anticlimax, so much so that churches have devised services for those who experience grief at this time of year. We need to celebrate even when there is little celebratory in us, and Advent makes room for that.

Advent

A single day simply does not suffice to take in the mystery of the incarnation and nativity, hence, the reason for Advent. Throughout the centuries, the definition and establishment of Christmas as a holy day continued to imply and emphasize the need to prepare so that it would not be missed, or "dissed"—not only calendar wise, but also spiritually. Christmas each year is a journey, and the preparation decides how rich a ride it will be. So, just as Christmas itself evolved as a consequence of yearning hearts, Advent, the four-week season prior to Christmas set apart as a time of devotion and reflection, took root as well.

Advent emanates historically from the observance of Christmas day as a first "coming" of Jesus. In fact, the name Advent comes from the Latin *adventus* which means, "a coming." *Adventus* translated the Greek word *parousia* which is used in scripture to refer to the Second Coming of Jesus or the recognition of His presence among us.

In liturgical churches, the traditions of Jesus' first and second comings were crafted and merged. During the first few centuries of Advent preparation, two weeks were given to focus upon the Second coming of Jesus and then two weeks were given to focus on His first coming. A preparation for His future coming and final judgement gave the Advent season a decidedly penitential bent with fasting at least three days per week as the day came closer. The church historically understood that Jesus came to be one of us but also comes now to live in us, dwelling in our hearts. And Jesus will still physically come again, this time to judge. Liturgical churches still do weekly readings in preparation for the second coming and final judgement. Yet, without denying the second coming, modern and post-modern churches have allowed the first coming to carry the weight of the holiday observance.

For most denominations Advent begins on the first of four Sundays counting back from Christmas itself. Evangelicals who observe Advent tend to follow that pattern. For Catholics, Advent begins with the Sunday which falls closest to November 30. Advent's four weeks for the process of preparation is a tradition observed for fifteen hundred years or so. Symbolic contrivances have risen to explain the number (such as each Sunday commemorating each writer of the Gospels), but most of this is the conjecture of afterthought. In the United States, Advent is sandwiched neatly between Thanksgiving and Christmas itself.

Attendant to the season is a host of accoutrements: carols, hymns, nativity scenes, plays, Christmas hangings, the building of the putz *(see note)*, the obligatory performance of Handel's

Messiah (although Handel had originally written it as an Easter piece), and of course the Advent wreath. Lutherans are the contributors of the Advent wreath tradition in the sixteenth century, constructing them of the same flora from Teutonic forests that gave us our Christmas tree and Christmas greens. Early wreaths were sometimes created with more than four candles--sometimes five or six. But four has become the norm in the church. The symbolism of each of the candles is multi-layered across different traditions, but the most popular meanings are faith, hope, joy and love, culminating in the lighting of the central candle on Christmas day. Each candle lit over four Sundays, of course, represents the light of the world having come and now brightening into the light of the world coming again. It is the Christmas sweep of redemptive history.

Those who are privileged to be at the manger have emptied themselves enough to recognize the arrival of a prince of peace, a prince who comes to enter our world, not merely conquer us.

These outward observances of Advent become deeply personal as we learn to ask the right questions of the season. What is the intention of observing Advent with respect to the human heart? What core attribute of God becoming incarnate can we ourselves seek and invest our hearts toward? Can we ask The Holy Spirit to recreate in us in some measure what Jesus modeled in coming to be one of us? What is the destination of these daily meditations and prayers? Is there a lesson in Advent's history?

Historically and theologically, the attribute of God sought in the Advent devotionals was and is humility. Groups as disparate as the Franciscans, the Jesuits, and the Mennonites in their formal Advent devotion all sought that same spiritual quality. However, the incarnate humility sought is not self-abasement nor self-abnegation. Rather, it is the authentic and simple manger species of humility, a particular sort of poverty that far exceeds material definitions of that word.

God in Jesus comes to us in such a way that we are not completely overwhelmed by His glory. All the power of the Godhead in heaven and earth comes in a manner that will not overpower us, modeling for us an emptying for the sake of authentic relationship. C.S. Lewis in *The Screwtape Letters* notes that God's presence is so vast that when He graces us with it, He does it in a merciful, measured way.[1] His presence is meted to us so as not to overpower us and negate our capacity to choose to receive Him. God never seeks a conquest, but rather a holy reception. Those who are privileged to be at the manger have emptied themselves enough to recognize the arrival of a prince of peace, a prince who comes to enter our world, not merely conquer us.

The spiritual direction, then, of a personal advent is to discover how to empty ourselves as the Son of God did. The ancients knew—and we need to rediscover—this sacred emptiness. It means that we willfully limit an insistent expression of our identity for the sake of love of God and of others, all the while maintaining an ease with who we are in Christ. This is the humility of the Son. When that humility is wrongly characterized as some form of sacrificial humiliation as some theologians have done, damage is done to the truth of who the Christ Child is.

Jesus emptied Himself of His divinity while remaining thoroughly divine. It was for the sake of relationship with us. His identity was perfectly intact and yet not asserted. We can learn the same humility. Devotions are the means whereby it is caught more than taught. This is the essence of Advent.

"Let each of you look not only to his own interests, but also to the interests of others. Have this mind among yourselves, which is yours in Christ Jesus, who, though he was in the form of God, did not count equality with God a thing to be grasped, but emptied himself, by taking the form of a servant, being born in the likeness of men." (Phil. 2:7)

Advent is our manger participation. Advent is about being

emptied so that the earth can be filled with the knowledge of God. God bless the twenty-five days and God bless you as you prepare along with us.

The Moravian Putz Tradition

The practice of the Moravian putz can be traced back to Europe when German and Alpine craftsmen began to carve figures of the Holy family from local native woods. Soon the finely carved Joseph and Mary were seen in churches, homes, and marketplaces. Moravians, immigrating to America in the eighteenth century, brought along some of the figures from their homelands. Early Moravians in America would prepare these displays and then go "putzing" to view fellow Moravians' displays in one another's homes.

The manger is always the center of any putz. Unlike a crèche, which depicts only a Nativity scene, a putz also includes some of the events prior to and following the birth of Jesus Christ—from Isaiah's prophecy and Mary's Annunciation, to the visit of the wise men and the flight into Egypt. Another distinctive feature is the inclusion of narration and lights in a Moravian putz to help tell the story. [2]

Letter One

1996 JOSEPH THE DREAMER

"She will bear a son and you shall call his name Jesus for he shall save his people from their sins." Matthew 1:21 NASB

THESE WORDS WERE VOICED to Joseph. They rumbled into his unconscious by the mouth of an angel - not in the same way that the angel had spoken to Mary. These words came in a dream. Joseph was dreaming a lot. On our dreamscapes truths arise that rationale will never deliver.

The girl to whom he pledged his life and love was pregnant. Joseph was not the father. No one knew who was. Save Mary! The depth of his love for her blocked his thoughts from publicly disgracing her. But he loved the Lord and the Torah too much to ignore what it seemed she had done. He didn't know it but he was facing his first Christmas. Fitful sleep often finds clarity in its dreams.

Like his namesake, this Joseph was a dreamer too. Crisis dreams loom large. We vividly track them. Maybe Joseph, the tradesman, remembered the dreams of Joseph, who dreamt his way into the court of Pharaoh. So, there are dreams that bear us to our destinies. And out of the blackness and turmoil of his nightmare, something preposterous was spoken—something only God would say. The child is not cursed. He is conceived of the Holy Spirit. And what you thought was the curse of sin would become the curse to sin itself.

More than that, the Father named Joseph as the earthly father of this child yet to be named. Name the baby and you are the father. Name this baby and Judah has a legitimate king. You will have a wife and a child like no other . . . ever.

From the first, Christmas, then, is a season to believe the God of our dreams. Whatever nightmares we harbor, what fears plague us, what turmoil haunts, God's choice of us will cause us to tromp on trouble, to dream our way through. May God speak into every burden this season and transform every family's predicament into its promise.

God's choice of us will cause us to tromp on trouble, to dream our way through.

This child named Jesus is the only reason why, despite the big nightmares across our world, sugar plum fairies dare dance in the heads of our little ones. Tricia and I and our family wish you a merry Christmas. And may your sleep be rest.

PRAYER:

Lord make me a dreamer for your kingdom. We thank You for angels yet invading our dreams. Where I see condemnation assaulting the ones I love, grant me the grace to love and to believe all things. Give to me your gift of discernment. Dispose me to be merciful as Joseph was thoroughly disposed toward Mary. During this season so many relationships resurface in our lives, good ones and difficult ones. Grant me the ability to recognize how good You are toward those I find difficult.

Jesus, I ask even at the beginning of the season that You unfold to me the wonder of the Christmas mystery. You became one of us, God made flesh. I commit to You the Advent days ahead. You know the distractions that we face during this time. Come Holy Spirit. Begin a Christmas preparation within me.

I offer to You those worries, those things that perplex me about your will and my place in your purposes. I pray especially for my family in this season oh God. Take some of the grace that You are putting on me and put it on them as well.

Give me a Kingdom estimate of those I love. Open my eyes to your work in them. Prepare my heart for a deepening awareness of how crazy the mystery is that we celebrate. Take me into this season dreaming the dreams of Zion. Amen.

Letter Two

---

*"Behold, the virgin shall be with child and shall bear a Son,
and they shall call His name Immanuel, which translated
means, God with us." Matthew 1:23 NASB*

THIS CRITICAL CHRISTMAS prophecy gives rise to a lot of
questions! Why virginity? Was it that the Father saw the virgin
womb as an exceptionally sacred place for His incarnate Son to
find form? Was the womb of Mary then a holier habitat simply
because she had not yet consummated her marriage? If so what
are the implications for all the rest of maternity? Why couldn't
Joseph have conceived the child with Mary? The Spirit then could
have infused the divine nature of the Son into the child? After all
miracles are miracles. How much easier would it have been on
Joseph? Despite that Matthew declares Mary's virginity to be the
fulfillment of what Isaiah had prophesied. Now there are "smart"
people who choose to believe the easier otherwise and make
Mary's virginity merely mythical. God's radical incarnate love,
however, can't be domesticated.

5

God's radical incarnate love, however, can't be domesticated.

The answer to the questions spring from the second half of the prophecy--- "God with us." When each of us asks the necessary question, "When did I come into being? What is the origin of who I am?" The answer is our conception. The ultimate origin of the baby Jesus was the unambiguous manifestation of God stirring life in the ovum of His "highly favored" one. Mary's "Be it unto me" leaves no obscure arrogance such that we understand ourselves to have engineered our own redemption.

Her virginity insures the pure life of a new creation man, a second Adam with none of the first Adam's sin bequeathed. In Mary's womb the promised seed of Eve and the overshadowing of the Holy Spirit, the created and the creator, the material and the immaterial are wed. It is an inaugural miracle. The child Messiah needed to be born first and born of Judah. Virgins are not holier than non-virgins. However, this particular virginity is the holy ground for the most supernatural and extraordinary conception of all births, leading forward and backward in history.

When a virgin bears a child it is no paradigm shift for virgins. It is a single, unique, unrepeated miraculous event. Isaiah declares that the virgin birth is sign. A sign of what? The virgin birth is a sign that God is disposed to do the preposterous, the uncommon, the thoroughly unique to accomplish His purpose in our lives.

The virgin birth is a sign that God is disposed to do the preposterous, the uncommon, the thoroughly unique to accomplish His purpose in our lives.

Trish and I and our family pray that this Christmas proves a time when you and your family find Jesus in some never before only-est sort of way. May you be wonderfully surprised as the

Incarnate One invades your Christmas and turns the mountain you thought insurmountable into a mountable one. And when you get to the top, say Merry Christmas to Immanuel.

PRAYER:

Lord Jesus, secure our hearts this season from the temptation to make your conception and birth somehow less than it is. Take all the other wonderful meanings of Christmas. Make them subservient to You alone. You alone are fully one of us and fully God. You alone are the new creation that we become as we live in You and have our being. So, Lord please don't let us confuse ourselves by the ambiguity that sets in when gifts and giving overshadow our most important gift . . . You oh God.

We want to revel in the impossibility of your virgin birth. We look to gain the receptivity of Mary's heart. When we think Isaiah's prophecy fulfilled, we know there is so much more that You intend to be fulfilled through us.

We believe that You are yet disposed to do the preposterous through us and in us. Make our hearts receptive as well. Give us an Advent season where the miraculous isn't just a memory. Let us see signs that create wonders even in hearts of stolid unbelievers.

Burden us Lord. Burden us this early with the lives of those we can invite to come with us as we celebrate the birth. Give us at our services, at our meals and at our prayers a ministry of the Holy Spirit that redeems, heals and brings hope. You love to sign so much, Jesus. You became the most impossible of signs, born to a virgin. Let this Christmas be a Christmas of signs signing You. Amen.

Letter Three

"So Joseph got up and took the Child and His mother while it was still night, and left for Egypt. He remained there until the death of Herod. This was to fulfill what had been spoken by the Lord through the prophet: "Out of Egypt I called My Son." Matthew 2:14-1 NASB

THIS IS the part of the Nativity story that doesn't make it to the front of the Christmas cards. Jesus, another refugee in Africa, another baby is imperiled by another lethal paranoid with an army at his disposal. As far as hell and Herod were concerned Christmas was war. Herod had already slaughtered two of his own sons whom he surmised to be contenders to his throne. Caesar Augustus said of Herod: "Better to be one of Herod's pigs than one of His sons."

So in Bethlehem a score of little ones died. One little one fled. That is the nightmare and the politics of the first Christmas. But to some, Christmas is yet construed as dangerous if it contains a rival throne to our own.

It begs a question. Why does the plan of God often appear to be in peril? Why is this baby King of Kings forced to find a safe place from the monster? Why all the strenuous protection, the running from darkness in darkness with the little Light of the World in tow? Matthew prophetically pegs a response from the words of the prophet Hosea. Just as Israel was sequestered out of its destiny for a while, so too would be its little King. It seems that chosen-ness, whether a chosen king or chosen people, carries a measure of refugee status with it. The Messiah is to identify with the mass of marginalized humanity on the earth.

> *The Messiah is to identify with the mass of marginalized humanity on the earth.*

In the West as Christmas's mercantile profile explodes, there are mean secularists who mean to strip from Christmas its meaning. So Christmas is still war. And littler less lethal monsters reduce the Incarnation to some tamed "happy holiday". As long as the little King, His God-ness, and His people stay in Egypt, hidden out of sight and over there somewhere, Christmas poses less of a threat. And we Christians become the refugees of our own holiday.

Maybe our marginalization is good. The Father seems from olden prophetic days intent to see His people identify with the marginalized of the world. So Trish and I pray that this Christmas, our worship, our celebration of Jesus, our joy, our faith and our prosperity would not be hidden from whatever fellow refugees and dispossessed ones come within reach of our love. As we enter a new millennium let them know that His love is our love. And the God who loves them is a refugee as well.

PRAYER:

From the first Jesus, You came among us to be marginalized by us. You identified with us that we might identify God in You.

10

Lord we pray for so very many marginalized people this season. Those whose lives are being scarred by war, hunger, homelessness, addiction . . . we pray for relief from whatever drives them to the margins of life and existence itself. Help them we pray and help us to help them. Help us not to forget that our holiday opulence serves as contrast to their squalor. God, bless our charities, our outreaches, our missions in a special way this season. Never let us forget that You came to be with us as a refugee.

We pray for those who hate You, who hate Christmas. We pray for those like Herod who have enthroned themselves and enthroned their own wills. They will not tolerate any rival throne in their lives. We ask you to break the back of their unbelief such that they cease to be instruments of darkness. God make this a season where we each see true Scrooges bend their knee and bow their heads to the King of Kings.

We recognize God that the nations are raging while You are on your throne, especially at this time. And when they rage, there are the victims of injustice, murder, fear. We pray for the victims but especially for the perpetrators as well.

Give each of us this day the door to be an instrument of your peace. Save us! Hosanna! Save them. Amen.

Letter Four

"... for He has been mindful of the state of His servant. From now on all generations will call me blessed, for the Mighty One has done great things for me—holy is his name." Luke 1:48 NIV

PREGNANT WOMEN CARRY a capacity to eek gratitude. Even in their complaints, when they are heavy with their load of life, and when the days to the birth are short with discomfort and lingering nausea; there is that shine that comes from them. It says, "somehow deep down where I am satisfied, I know I was born to do this." In its English roots the word, woman, means 'man-with-a-womb.' We men without wombs unfortunately don't seem to have any comparable anatomy that yields the same shine, that same thankfulness. We daren't tell our women that their faces should shine with that pregnant glow. But It just happens!

The words quoted above are the words of an especially pregnant Hebrew girl, Mary. As she erupts into this praise for God, she looks forward to misunderstandings, accusations, confusion, the jeopardy of her fiancé's abandonment, the jeopardy of single

13

motherhood in a culture where single motherhood is just less than a death sentence. Of course, there is the danger of childbirth itself. And yet here she is shining away, exuding this gratitude toward God. She is convinced. She is bearing a Savior to a very lost, perishing world.

We can bear the life of Christ into the same darkness into which she bore Jesus.

One reason that Mary is called "blessed" by all of us, then, is because her pregnancy is one we all can get in on—whether we have wombs or not. Her shine can be our shine. We can bear the life of Christ into the same darkness in which she bore Jesus. For many, Christmas is a season where expectations run high and reality lies low. On behalf of Tricia and me, we propose that, this season, we all get in this business of birthing Christ into someone's life. . . and we propose . . . that we all shine too.

PRAYER:

Oh to be able. . . to carry the Christ to even one of all the many in need of You Lord especially right now! Mary is our model . . . Holy Spirit make us pregnant as well. Have us put a shine on even as Mary shined with your presence? We want to carry You and birth You in the life of someone else this season. We need eyes to see the who, the when and the where. But first we need eyes to see that because of your apprehension of each of us, we too are "full of grace." We too are blessed.

At your conception, Jesus, Mary sang her song as if you were already on the throne at the right hand of the Father. She worshipped into the future of the world. But for us You ARE on the throne at the right hand of the Father. Make us to sing and pray with the same faith.

In the face of all the real and potential hazards we are facing, we will rebuke them with that same faith . . .lay the threats aside, worship You for your ever-present regard of us. We thank You for saving us and we look to sing our salvation songs through this season to our celebration of the Birth of our salvation. Make it be a season for divine appointments to be had . . . new births to be gained. Amen.

Letter Five

2002 DON'T BE AFRAID

"Do not be afraid . . . for today in the city of David there has been born for you a Savior who is Christ the Lord. This will be a sign for you: you will find a Baby wrapped in cloths and lying in a feeding trough." Luke 2:10-12 NASB

A BEMUSING SIGHT! The Shepherds are afraid while Christmas becomes our most sublime reason not to be afraid any more. Two things the shepherds needed to know from angels. Don't be afraid . . . and . . . today a Savior. The today of Christmas lies at a time between times in almost all calendars always. It lies at the genesis of a new, frightening human history, the upcoming year, as opposed to the old frightening history - the previous year. We can make that claim any year because no years are not frightening.

An angel said something to shepherds two thousand years ago as they were tucking in their sheep. And it is a sentiment for us. The angel didn't ask but commanded them: "don't be afraid." Those days were just as violent as ours. There was terrorism, vicious warlords, a brutal, occupying army, narcissistic leaders.

God invades fear with His wonderful childlikeness, His foolishness that confounds the wise. To combat human failure and disappointment God sends what looks like His utter vulnerability.

God invades fear with His wonderful childlikeness, His foolishness that confounds the wise.

The greatest redemption plan of cosmic history snores little redemption snores in a feeding troth. The more enormous the threat, the less the Holy One of Israel needs to flex muscle. We fearful ones merely need the presence of a wee Godman.

This Christmas season, like every season since the first one, we need to find our today Savior. So, we move through a season with tinsel and Christmas charms juxtaposed to media ever traipsing before us various nightmares of humanity frightened of itself. Make the effort in the hubbub to see the sign. The Father's plan to save us from predicaments is usually camouflaged in seeming inadequacy, vulnerability, impossibility. It is in that meekness that Jesus arrives to exercise His enormous power to redeem.

Now each of us is to nourish those who are so deeply disappointed and blind to God's foolishness. I call it manger presence! May God give us the wisdom of the angel to say, "We won't be afraid." Then may God give us the guilelessness of the shepherd to bring ourselves and others to the place of His redeeming today presence. In such a way, every day is Christmas. On behalf of Trish and me and my family may this season find you with the today Savior.

PRAYER:
Jesus, today You are our Savior. Today! The angels announced "...today a Savior." And all of hell heard the declaration as well. Not yesterday! Not tomorrow! A Savior for today.

As we hear the reports of murder and chaos and confusion that menacingly dance across the medias, today we are not afraid. As we regard the hazards that life causes us to face; the sickness, the misunderstanding, the fractured relationships, the lovelessness of a lost world in all of its manifestations; today we are not afraid. When our enemy would have us catalogue all of the evil that just might and could happen, today we are not afraid. Because a Savior has been born for us and He is on His throne today!

Jesus as we acknowledge and thank You that through last year your manger presence was ever immanent to guide us, to keep us through thick and thin. So, we lean into the new year by celebrating your manger presence. You who were unafraid in a world as dangerous as ours, be our today Savior through each day of this new year. We look to fear You such that no other fear would ever overtake us. In your name!

Letter Six

2003 THE MAGI BECOME WISE

Magi from the east came to Jerusalem and asked, "Where is the one who has been born king of the Jews? We saw his star in the east and have come to worship him. When King Herod heard this . . . he had called together all the people's chief priests and teachers of the law, he asked them where the Christ was to be born. In Bethlehem in Judea," they replied, "for this is what the prophet has written . . ." Matthew 2:1-5: NIV

IN CONTRAST to those who are often considered to be wise in our culture, the wise men who graced the first Christmas were wise for other reasons. When they saw the light, they followed the light. They didn't merely study the light, track it, bask a bit in its star shine. They didn't merely acknowledge that a special light existed. They realized at some level, that it was unlike other lights. It stirred up a yearning to follow it. It was moving and it was leading them. And they let the light take them somewhere new and risky. They followed the light on a quest.

What especially made them wise was their comprehension of

the limitations of the light. The light was wonderful and had moved them a long way. But in and of itself, it would not take them all the way to the manger. The light caused them to inquire of the scriptures. The direction of the light was submitted to the word of God, to "what the prophet has written." It was then that these Magi became Christmas wise. They saw what the supposedly wisest of the world were blind to. They found what the religious wise chose to ignore. They brought gifts to a little king who is God incarnate.

> *The light was wonderful and had moved them a long way. But in and of itself, it would not take them all the way to the manger.*

I trust that this Christmas finds us all following hard after the light which has been given to us. I trust that, in the submission of our hopes to God's word, we find ourselves on a quest, worshipping the King of Truth, Jesus. On behalf of Trish and me, may you encounter a Christmas filled with light and truth and . . . a quest.

PRAYER:

Our Lord, our Light! When most of the world which You came to save remained ignorant of even your coming, the very cosmos responded to the birth of the King. When the religious, when those who claimed to be awaiting You were paralyzed from even considering You, Gentiles chose to follow your light.

We have seen your light. Despite that we too often ask ourselves, "Just where are we going in this life we live, this faith walk . . . when our light seems to, just like that, disappear for a moment?

We will follow You wherever your light goes. But we only want to follow where You lead Lord. Like the Magi we submit whatever light we may glean to the Word of God. Then we know we will arrive at the truth. Jesus You are the truth and the light. Therefore, You are our way as well. As we pray and we worship through this season into the new year. Lead us oh Lord. Take us on a journey to the increase of your Kingdom . . . Take us into the heart of hope . . . beyond what we can ask or think. Amen!

Letter Seven

"Today . . . was born to you a Savior which is Christ the Lord." Luke 2:11 NASB

THE PARADOX of the angel's declaration should floor us. This infant who is Savior and Lord and Christ, who will walk on water, must also toddle. This infant who is, at once, all that He was and all that He will be must learn to crawl. Thirty years before he falls on the Via Dolorosa, he must take tumbles like the rest of us on our way to walking. This baby who will one day heal the sick is vulnerable to viruses and homicidal kings. The Word made flesh must learn to speak words.

The angel pointedly did not say, "And this child will grow to be a Savior of His people" . . . or something such. Most saviors have boundaries. They are attached to nations and peoples and states. Most saviors are born and then grow up *to be* saviors. Our Savior was born our Savior whether Jew or Gentile. The angel's words are clear, baby simple. The babe born is a Savior. The babe born is the Christ.

At the moment that Mary responded to the angel Gabriel and received the holy implosion in her womb, Jesus is saving us. His conception, His gestation, His travel down the birth canal, the blood and the pain, the first breath, the first searching suckle at His mother's breast, all of it was part of His saving act. This manger scene can't be cutely parceled out apart from humanity's desperate need of a Savior. The crucified Jesus reaches us from His mother's womb to His tomb.

Why then should it be surprising to us that our salvation comes to us through a birth as well?

So then, our Savior came to us through a birth. Why then should it be surprising to us that our salvation comes to us through a birth as well? Because He was born, may the celebration of His birth find us, each one of us this Christmas, born again!

On behalf of Tricia and me, may the Christmas baby be known by you as the Christmas Savior.

> *"Man's maker was made man that He, Ruler of the stars, might nurse at His mother's breast; that the Bread might hunger, the Fountain thirst, the Light sleep, the Way be tired on its journey; that Truth might be accused of false witnesses, the Teacher be beaten with whips, the Foundation be suspended on wood; that Strength might grow weak; that the Healer might be wounded; that Life might die."*
> - Saint Augustine

PRAYER:
Lord we beseech You that in all of our festivities, the froth and the tinsel of this season, even in the carols and worship times, we will never lose for a moment the truth that You are Savior. You saved us. You are saving us. You will save us. You save those whom we love. You save your enemies . . . our enemies.

Please, oh Lord Christ, baptize this very season into the salvation for which You were conceived and born even from before the foundation of the world. All glory and power and praise are yours. Save us oh God!

Letter Eight

2005 FULLNESS OF TIME

"In the same way we also, when we were children, were enslaved to the elementary principles of the world. But when the fullness of time had come, God sent forth his Son, born of woman, born under the law, to redeem those who were under the law..." Galatians 4:3-5 ESV

WHAT ON EARTH does it mean to say that time experienced a fullness, became complete? What kind of ripened time gives rise to the manger? What "elemental things of the world" enslave us until the world's capacity for bondage is reached? It is sin's harvest that packs time. . . death, violence, injustice, devastation. And then the search for meaning. Those kinds of things. So heaven saw humanity reduced to its dreary dilemma. We are beyond saving ourselves. We need a Savior who is and isn't one of us.

From the time when Malachi ceased to prophesy and the Old Testament was closed until the nativity of the Christ and the New Testament was opened, there lies the conspicuous gap. Scholars have named it the great silence. It is as if God had said, "OK girls and boys, let's see what you got?" And then God hushed and watched as history made a parade.

All of the Pharisaic huffing and puffing in attempts to fulfill the law couldn't do the trick of salvation. Oh and the Gentiles, we huffed and puffed as well. People asked the best questions. There were the likes of Socrates, Aristotle, Plato. Oh yes and Buddha, Confucius, Lao Tzu, Zoroaster, and others. They all ultimately in their varying ways saw salvation grounded in what we do.

And we all, Jews first then Gentiles, gave it our best huffing and puffing. God gave us four hundred years of time so that time itself could burst with our own impotent exhaustion. But . . . time became pregnant as well. In a dusty corner of the world, God gave us His best. An anonymous little virgin bore and lay in a manger the only ultimate answer, the only way, God Himself! Born under the law of Moses and under the law of a universe groaning and travailing as it rushes toward chaos, the squall of the baby Jesus entered where we live. Heaven didn't respond with propositions or practices. Christmas is the celebration of God responding with incarnate life.

Heaven didn't respond with propositions or practices.

During this season as manger scenes and carols bring on those questions that no philosophy can completely answer. Can we take our cues from Jesus? More than reasoning our way into the hearts of others, can we love our way there? Maybe find the Father's ways to offer our lives to those in need of Him which, by the way, means they are in need of us as well.

PRAYER:
The goodness of your fatherhood, Lord God, never ceases to stagger us. You create us out of your love. And then you seek to

actually enter what You created. You are the cosmic artist who marches into His canvas to address every imperfection with glory. Jesus, we revel in the realization that You are not just similar to us. You have become one of us in the fullness of time.

There is a fullness of time for history, for the world itself, for the kingdom of darkness. Each of us personally, inevitably discovers ourselves to be in a fullness of time as well. Each of us comes to our ultimate pertinent moment. Our time to finally become intact by the power of your love. We too easily say, "I found Jesus." But the truth is that Jesus, You found us.

Thank You God for numbering the days, hours and minutes of our lives to bring us to this "fullness of time." Thank you, Father, for sending Your Son. Thank You Holy Spirit for ministering the grace to receive Him. Thank You that we are able to rise out of the dreariness of this world to become new creations.

Grant grace to anyone reading this prayer who has yet to find their time to be full, to recognize You, receive You, and ascend to that fullness this Christmas season. So good a God! So much to be realized!

So, each year, this year, we cheer your birth . . . praise incarnate life come among us to save us. But more . . . to render us into a new creation now destined for a never ending, new world without endings. Amen!

great

is

the

lord

Stecker

Letter Nine

2006 HUMILITY IS NOT HUMILIATION

"But the angel said to them, "Do not be afraid. I bring you good news of great joy that will be for all the people . . . Suddenly a great company of the heavenly host appeared with the angel, praising God and saying, "Glory to God in the highest, and on earth peace to men on whom his favor rests." Luke 2:10-14 NIV

THE CHRISTMAS PERFORMANCES that punctuate our churches' advent seasons typically begin with a portrayal of the Incarnation. And it goes something like this; The place is heaven. The characters are God the Father and God the Son. The Father commissions the Son to become one of us, to become the baby Jesus sent into a world of suffering and woe. And the mood of the Father is sober and serious at the cost of it all. As it is played, heaven is somber as if Christmas, at its heart, is the beginning of the great contingency plan. Heaven is being emptied. And there is a sense that the darling of heaven is coerced by our sin to go to be among those whom He loves but with whom He, in His divinity, does not really belong. It's as if His emptying of Himself is the great condescension.

The problem is that scripture declares a heaven with a radically different perspective on that first Christmas. When the Shepherds peer into heaven they see a virtual aurora borealis of joy and praise. No grief among those angels whatsoever! Just glory! From heaven's perspective there is nothing less than the celebration of the ultimate homecoming. Dare we assume less from the Father? The God who walked in the cool of Eden's days with the first family has come to be with the family again, to transform that family as He intended from before the foundation of the cosmos.

It is the prototype homecoming motif for all of the art and the endless episodes of loved ones returning home to family on Christmas.

The humility with which God became one of us was not, for God, a humiliation. No. It was a forever intended joy. And the nativity is, from the first, God's family plan. It is the prototype homecoming motif for all of the art and the endless episodes of loved ones returning home to family on Christmas. God, in the baby Jesus, has come to be with whom He belongs and with whom he planned to belong—from forever. Emmanuel is God with us in the flesh for forever.

On behalf of myself and Tricia, we pray that, this Christmas, you find your homecoming in Christ because Jesus has found a home in you.

Prayer:

Really God! Who on earth and in heaven are we? You are mindful of us? More than that, You are enamored of us! What is this sacred foolishness?

Jesus, when You became us, You injected a measure of your

glory into the humanity You created. Despite our sin, our imperfection, the extent of our degradation, it was your design . . . before You founded the world . . . to ultimately see to it that nothing of your birth, death and resurrection would be squandered. You render to your redeemed a dignity and power before angels and devils that just changes everything.

Jesus, for those who know You and embrace You yet still demean themselves, open the eyes of their hearts to see You for who You are and who they are in You. Let the light flood in so they understand that there is a hope in their calling. Because it is for the fulfillment of your work in us that heaven rejoices and glorifies You.

For those who don't know You, we ask for them to gain their sight of the God-respect awaiting them. We pray for Christmas gifts of holy perception, especially to so many downcast of soul. Enlighten our heart's eyes. During this season enlighten the heart's eyes of families to the gift that they are to one another . . . to the dignity that they carry because of your incarnation. Give all of us the ability to see what the angels saw and proclaimed to the shepherds. Amen.

Letter Ten

2007 ACCORDING TO HIS WORD

"And behold, Elisabeth thy kinswoman, she also hath conceived a son in her old age; and this is the sixth month with her that was called barren. For no word from God shall be void of power. And Mary said, Behold, the handmaid of the Lord; be it unto me according to thy word."
Luke 1:36-38 ASV

HUMAN WORDS CARRY A POWER. They shape perceptions, sometimes for good, sometimes for bad. We fish for impressions. "What's the word on him? What's the word on her? The "word" on Elizabeth was that she was barren. This meant in her culture that, at best, she was terribly unfortunate or, at worst, she was simply cursed.

God's Word on us bears a different kind of power. God's words create reality. They turn life upside down. Elizabeth received God's word and, just like that, she who was characterized as cursed is now she who is miracle-blessed in her old age. God's word does the impossible and overturns a lifetime of misunderstanding. Would that we all have our lives turned upside down by the power of a word from God—in the manner of Elizabeth!

God's words create reality.
They turn life upside down.

But the "word" that was out on Mary was a different matter. She was young. She was fortunate. She was a virgin due soon to finalize her marriage to a righteous man. And God's word is borne to her to turn her life upside down as well. God's word for Mary bears all kinds of jeopardy. Young, unwed and pregnant, she could have been launched into a life of misunderstanding. Called cursed. Nevertheless, she said "yes" to the word from God. For herself, for all of us, she said "yes". During this season, as each of us will be challenged by the truth of a babe in a manger, a word from God made flesh.

It is my deepest hope that each of us will say yes to that Word, Jesus Christ. It's Tricia's and my own hope that we say yes despite the promise or the peril. Because this Word from God is never ever void of power! So from the both of us, may it be unto all of us according to His word.

PRAYER:

On the first Christmas, God, You spoke your Word, through Gabriel, to Mary. Our world was made topsy-turvy from that time forward. God became man and a man is God. Jesus! There are so many of us, like Mary and Elizabeth who need our worlds turned topsy turvy for the increase of your Kingdom.

Make us to be Christmas vessels. We want to create hope this season so that the disillusioned, depressed, the ambivalent, even the faithless see that things can really change. Angels can be dispatched with words from God, directed into the human heart. A word from God is not, for a moment, void of power. Lord if we need to, we will be your angels, your messengers. We are at your service, and at the service of your words. For Mary, Elizabeth's topsy turvy was confirmation that her own topsy turvy was real. She knew for sure. God her Redeemer was using her for the redemption of the world. Render to us Holy Spirit words for the season that turn worlds upside down. Release the power of Jesus Christ come among us. There is, in the pomp and circumstance of the season, a world rendered silent or deaf to words from God. Lord make us to break the glass-ceiling irony of that. Words need to be heard, Holy Spirit. So that even as He has become, His kingdom comes. Amen.

Letter Eleven

2008 SACRED PLACE

"When Elizabeth heard Mary's greeting, the baby leaped in her womb; and Elizabeth was filled with the Holy Spirit. And she cried out with a loud voice and said, "Blessed are you among women, and blessed is the fruit of your womb!"
Luke 1:41-42 NASB

THROUGHOUT THE HISTORY of redemption God chooses His sacred places, space set apart for us to worship Him. From the sweet devotion that characterized David's tabernacle, to the adorned majesty of Solomon's temple, He set the place. Herod's architects and slaves strove to make a wonder of the worship world atop Zion. But what crazy prophet would have dreamt that the most sublime tabernacle in all of Israel ultimately would be a mere womb that cradled the little one, a virgin's womb at that. For Mary and Elizabeth and John the Baptist, the womb is the place. The place for life, not just life in the womb, but God's life! The place of first worship! The place of the fellowship of these unborn! The place where fetal lovers of God incite their mothers to testimony and joy and praise!

And we work to create our sacred places as well, Christmas churches and Christmas households—poinsettias and mangers and lights and tinsel. We look to frame the joy of the season. But above church or temple or cathedral, when the Father chose the first sacred place for His incarnate son to be adored, He chose a womb. And the intensity of the presence of God in a womb evoked a burst of joy and adoration in another womb.

But above church or temple or cathedral, when the Father chose the first sacred place for His incarnate son to be adored, He chose a womb.

During this Christmas season may we be conscious of this, *the sanctity of a filled womb*. And may we be conscientious to pray that the same God who fills a womb with a life, will fill those wombs with His presence and His joy and His security and His protection.

On behalf of Trish and me, may the wish and will of the season be that we live in a world where filled wombs are sacred places.

PRAYER:

Jesus, You became an unborn one first. You were conceived. You gestated. You entered a birth canal. You cried and you suckled your mother's breast. You escaped the swinging scalpels of Herod's soldiers as they murdered the holy innocents of Bethlehem. Yet none was more innocent than You.

This season especially God, even as angels protected You within the dreams of Joseph, protect the unborn, Lord. The little ones whose path You chose to imitate. Regard them and regard those impoverished mothers who struggle with all of their hearts and souls. They see their children from desperation, an oppressive responsibility for whom they have no resource. Give them eyes to see their little ones because they see You. Give us the grace to respond to their destitution of heart . . . in real terms . . . in kingdom terms.

Thank You for coming to save us in such frailty. Save us. Save them. Save us all. Hosanna in the highest. Hosanna for the lowest. Amen!

Letter Twelve

And Mary said:

"My soul glorifies the Lord and my spirit rejoices in God my Savior, for he has been mindful of the humble state of his servant. From now on all generations will call me blessed ..." Luke 1:46-48 NIV

DURING THE FIRST CHRISTMAS, the angel Gabriel was sent twice. He came to Zacharias, a priest in the temple in Jerusalem, to declare that God was giving him a son. And then he visited Mary, a Jewish virgin teen, not religiously special, from nowhere religiously important. Zacharias' unbelieving response to the angel ends in imposed silence. Mary's response culminates in the first Christmas song. And it is one lyrical eruption of joy in which she sings that God turns everything around by means of His favor. In the most personal way she declares God to be her own Savior.

What does she mean, her Savior? There is the big sense that she was numbering herself as one of Israel inasmuch as all Israel needed to be saved. Yet Israelites certainly had different notions as to what kind of saving was essential.

But there is a more pragmatic sense of the need for saving here. And it is more immediate and simple and personally dangerous than redeeming the nation. She has just journeyed eighty miles into the Judean mountains as she was instructed by Gabriel. She will return home alone and three months pregnant with Jesus. She is, to be sure, in some fix.

She faces the scorn of a village and, no doubt, the astonishment of a husband, Joseph, who has not as yet dreamed his redemptive dreams. She is, at this point, a single mother facing arduous journeys, accusations, the possibility of divorce, taxation, deportation, a maniac king and his assassins, and finally, refugee status. She needs a Savior.

And yet she has this song. Her lyrics extoll the faithfulness of a God who turns our predicaments to praise; a God who reverses everything with His favor. And her hope pivots upon humility and the willingness to sing.

This year has been a year of dilemma for many. A year of surprising and entrenching fixes, jobs lost, health insurance issues, and gritty disappointments all around. But this is not the season for a silence. Rather, may our problems become fuel, this season, to see and to sing like a virgin with a womb full of hope. Can we sing acknowledging that in God every predicament packs a promise. Who knows? We, too, may bear the Christ to someone who is far more lost and in a fix.

On behalf of Trish and me, we wish you a very merry season of His regard and his favor.

PRAYER:

Father God, You seem to have engineered Christmas for singing. But Christmas never was for singing our way through neutral circumstances. You designed Christmas as paths of joy, but through the inevitable fixes of our lives. As we consider the challenges we all face this Advent. As we consider the far more monumental challenges that others face. We want to sing salvation songs. Like Mary we want our songs to be prophetic of your future goodness toward us and those whom we love . . . those whom we should love.

Show us how to tend to those who feel trapped. Even as Elizabeth harbored a pregnant mother who was facing all manner of misunderstanding and danger. Give us the resources, the grace to be intentional to those who need us and who ultimately need You.

Keep us mindful of our humility and let every carol be filled with hope and creative grace. We pray especially for those facing the impossible. Mary faced impossible situations and yet she sang salvation songs. We believe that You Lord will make every predicament yield a promise this season. As we worship in our churches and our homes and in the streets let the world hear, through the din, music of salvation. Amen!

Letter Thirteen

2010 THE FUSS IN BEING FAVORED

"Now in the sixth month the angel Gabriel was sent from God to a city in Galilee called Nazareth, to a virgin . . . And coming in, he said to her, "Greetings, favored one! The Lord is with you." But she was very perplexed at this statement, and kept pondering what kind of salutation this was." Luke 1:26-30 NASB

OVER THE CENTURIES, scholars have traded opinions on what it was that Gabriel had said that actually troubled Mary so much. It would be understandable if it was his appearance that struck her. Here we have the same angel, the sight of whom "gripped" Zechariah "with fear" and ultimately rendered him speechless six months earlier. But the text is clear. Mary's trouble lay in the simple words the angel spoke. This was not a rapid dialogue. She "kept pondering the kind of salutation." Mary was not naïve. Mary was a thinker.

Two sayings disturbed her deeply. The first was the declaration of her favor in the sight of God. What was the nature of this "favor?" Did he mean that she was favored consequent to something that she did? Was it her behavior, her character, her relationship with Him? Or was the favor the sovereign choice of God? Was she favored for what she would do? Was she favored in the sense that it was yet to be manifest? Was she a mere human vessel flooded with grace? In this pondering we have millennia of arguments about the nature of grace bouncing about in a Galilean girl's heart.

But perhaps more disturbing was this question. "What kind" of greeting was this? What were its intentions? What destiny and implications lay in the seed of this Hail Mary? What would this greeting introduce to her life? Mary was a student. Her agility in freely singing scriptures declares it. From the scriptures she knew His chosen champions. They were also "favored" of God. With God's favor comes joy. But with favor the joy carries its own jeopardy. It meant that the joy of being chosen would be followed with responsibility for the Grace given.

It meant that the joy of being chosen would be followed with responsibility for the Grace given.

She was preparing herself for the inevitable next words of the angel. Mary was a mother. Her decision would require sacrifice and selflessness, suffering injustice, a willingness to be accused, misunderstood. Smart kid! The child would emulate the child she would bear.

Are we prepared to authentically keep pondering the Christmas truth? Because Mary pondered, each of us is now chosen. Each has been immensely favored. And with the joy of this season comes jeopardy. That grace given to us demands, that in turn, we bear the sacrificial cost of offering Jesus to a lost world.

Tricia and I, along with our children and our children's children wish that, this Christmas, all who ponder the salutation of Gabriel are likewise favored of the Lord. May we be likewise joyous, and likewise willing to take on board the responsibility of the call.

PRAYER:

God, we realize that inasmuch as we are in the process of praying right now, it is a sign that we have already been favored by You. You give us grace to believe in you, a God who loves us and responds to our prayers. But we also understand something else. We regard those other saints that journey through the story of your birth. For them, to be chosen is to receive grace, to be favored is to be called, then to face the responsibility attached to grace given.

Jesus, You have given us so very much. The giving of your life is why we give the gifts at this season. You gave your very life on our behalf. To whom much is given, You expect much. So then the cost of your favor toward us is this obedience we are to move in. Tell us what to do. A word we need that is full, never void of power! This word of yours is a sweet and savory burden.

Just as Mary pondered the salutation of Gabriel, we are pondering the grace You have filled us with. We ask for hearts to fulfill the obedience required of us. We want to say, 'be it unto us according to your Word.' We want to see miracles this season even as Mary did. As we walk out the obedience, yield to your grace, give us Christmas glimmers of the miraculous. Instead of the glint of so much tinsel and electric light, give us a gleam of heaven. That will be enough! Amen.

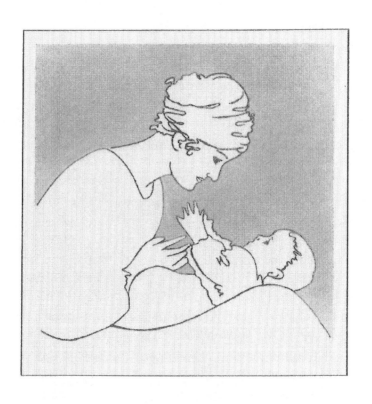

Letter Fourteen

2011 THE OFFENSE OF A MANGER BABE

"When they saw the star, they rejoiced exceedingly with great joy. After coming into the house they saw the child and Mary, His mother and they fell to the ground and worshipped Him. Then opening their treasures they presented to Him gifts... " Matt. 2:10-11 NASB

WHY IS it the intention of some to limit the joy of Christmas, to dial down the intensity of the star? The first "war on Christmas" that I remember was actually declared by some evangelical Christians. I recall Grinch-like mumblings and constipated looks. They warned us about pagan Christmas trees, inexact dates, and yes, worldly religion. And I smelled fear. It was the fear that others might celebrate the incarnation of Jesus without arriving at that complete understanding of the gospel which, after all, they possessed. Christmas, they surmised, was something that those in the world could use to let themselves off the redemptive hook. The threat of Christmas was that the joy might confuse sinners.

These days the "war on Christmas" is carried out by the inclusive marketing minions. Herod's soldiers! Their swords slash away at the child. They monitor the Christmas language, assault the art to erase any remembrance. The seed truth that God is with us should never again decorate those department store doors. Carols of the Son are cut away for glitzy songs of silence. After all, their mandate is to protect the Christmasless from the offense of any starshine.

But here is what is fascinating. Both wars are prosecuted by those who, at heart, are offended by a babe in a manger—the irresistible perfection that the very God of the universe arrives in all vulnerability and meekness. The fact that God did not come to threaten us, threatens us.

Christmas is ultimate inclusiveness. The ultimate invitation! These magi from Matthew's gospel were as gentile as gentile could be. From the religious leaders' perspective, they were unchosen and unbelievers. Yet here we have them believing away. They were believing unbelievers. And no one was embarrassed. At Christmas, our churches are salted with them—gentiles are us— those who typically refrain from any expression of faith or worship at any other time. Yet, at Christmas, they come. Oh, they disguise their coming with masks of family obligation and tradition. But God knows the real reason they come. Some part of them hopes. If they follow the light there really may be the perfect gift to be had.

So, invite the believing unbelievers to Christmas! Be their star.

So, invite the believing unbelievers to Christmas! Be their star. And simply because they come, don't ask yourself or them where they have been. Dial up the brightness. Be intent on sharing the joy. And simply because they come, they may find the perfect gift as well!

Tricia and I, along with our family, wish you the very

brightest of Christmas light and the wisdom to follow it into this new year.

PRAYER:

God, we ask You to anoint with the gladness of your Holy Spirit all of these planned occasions for our season. Saturate our schedules. We pray for our church services, for our homes, the times of gathering, the parties and hospitality. You gave the Magi just enough starshine to bring them to the manger king.

Give the teeming number of unbelieving believers that meander through this time enough starshine to discover who You are. Whether they are family or friends or acquaintances, bring them on. Show them a gleam of the Holy Spirit, put a yearning in their hearts to really discover what the Christmas fuss is really about.

But prepare each of us for them then. Guide us through these Advent devotions, this journey to the holy day. Keep us from holiday squabbles, from yielding to financial worries, all of those things that so easily cloud our joy. Prepare us with the Christmas truth and the path to communicate it well. Bring to us, these figurative Gentiles.

We need to freely give as we have freely been given . . . whatever those gifts that the needy need . . . whether spiritual or physical. As they discover the truth of Emmanuel, that God is with us in You, show them that they carry the greatest treasure they can offer. This Christmas they can give their hearts to You. Amen,

Letter Fifteen

2012 THE OLD AND NEW ORDER TOUCH

---

*"When Elizabeth heard Mary's greeting, the baby leaped
in her womb; and Elizabeth was filled with the Holy Spirit.
And she cried out with a loud voice..." Luke 1:41-42 NASB*

THE WAY that historians construct things, when one age of
history draws to a close, the next age, that perfidious new one,
inevitably clashes with the old. Sometimes the collision is violent
—new thinking, new values, new culture, new norms. What are
things coming to? So we have the "Dark" ages succumbing to the
rise of an "Enlightenment." We have the post-modern trouncing
the modern. That is the back and forth of human history. God's
history is different. There is no back and forth. His history is
seamless in purpose. It confounds the experts. It finds understanding and expression in the hearts and souls of the mothers
who carry their children.

In the wombs of Mary and Elizabeth lie the pregnancy of
both an old order and a new one—an old covenant and a new.
John, the greatest of the old and Jesus, whose wonder is beyond

the anticipation of Israel. *But no tension between the babies!* God changes ages more delicately than experts could know. He does it in mangers and garden tombs. An old mother to be and a young mother embrace. The bellies of pregnant mothers rub and the old age kisses the new one. When the old experiences the new we have in utero Pentecost. Old moms, young moms and babies are filled with the Holy Spirit. Every mother thrills at the stirring of life in her womb. But Elizabeth feels the first prophecy of John as he declares with a kick the coming of his cousin, Messiah. Mary and Elizabeth understand that they are both wonder-full. And they realize they are expecting in more ways than one. Hope and promise and destiny are the hallmarks as God swings His seasons.

And they realize they are expecting in more ways than one. Hope and promise and destiny are the hallmarks as God swings His seasons.

This has been a year in which we continue to be assaulted. Hand wringing prognostications, prophecies, predictions and endings of the world allow little room at the inn for God's pregnant promises. But the obstinate fact remains that it is Christmas. A child wonder was born two thousand years ago. We live in a culture desperate for an Elizabeth and a Mary, both old and young to be pregnant with hope and promise.

To that end, as we gather with our families and friends these holidays and peer into a new year's empty canvass, can our mindset be: "With what new expression of His love is God's Kingdom pregnant?" May our tables and times be decorated with declarations of our hope, a pregnancy of God's favor toward a desperate world? Tricia and I and our family wish you the deepest Merry Christmas as we celebrate the One of wonders, Christ with us.

PRAYER:

Lord Jesus, this season and this coming year, intervene, save us from the clash of generations. Make yourself known to a new generation as You have done again and again. Befuddle the medias and all of the prognosticators that seem to celebrate the demise of the truth in Christmas. We refuse to accept that a new order is arising, a new generation bereft of You. Cause the arrogance of those who reject You to be turned into astonishment. Cause them to see the new order and the old order rejoice . . . just as the unborn Jesus and the unborn John swooned in the wombs of their mothers.

Give those of us who are older the grace to allow our profiles to decrease. Give the younger ones grace to accept You and all that your kingdom offers to a deeply needy humanity . . . in humility. And grant to the young that their profiles increase even as your Kingdom within them does.

For so many who are loathe to come to holiday worship but do so merely for the sake of politeness or family, enlighten them. Let the Spirit of God that created the carols, the liturgies, the prayers, the performances, break through and capture the hearts of another generation. Do it again. Amen.

Letter Sixteen

2013: THE SPLITTING OF THE ADAM

"JESUS, when He began his ministry . . . being as was supposed the son of Joseph . . . the son of Adam, the son of God." Luke 3:23, 38 NASB

EXCLUSIVELY, TWO INDIVIDUALS IN ALL OF THE scriptures are privileged to bear that specific title "the son of God." One of these, Adam, was created by his Father. The other was begotten not made. Saint Paul calls Him the second Adam— in a manner after his ancestor. Christmas is the feast in which we celebrate the splitting of the Adam. In this fission of the Father's wisdom, light and power and grace detonate within the first cries of a newborn baby laid in a manger. There is no arrogant flash, no cloud, nor primeval roar. Only songs of angels and shepherds! The silent sweep of a guiding star that captivates outlying astronomers to a town called Bethlehem on the margins of nowhere!

Yet the fabric of everything changes. Grace is unleashed. Mercifully, nothing is ever the same. The old atoms, the carbons and hydrogens and oxygens too, all those elements that compose each human being, were perfectly fused, flesh and God bonded whole. The valence of a virgin's faith pushed hard and a new Adam emerged bloody from her womb and into our earth. And suddenly it becomes needful that we trace our own selves to the miracle of it and of Him.

Jesus, like us, is the product of two—family trees. Matthew's gospel gives us Joseph's and Luke follows up with Mary's. But the lists of names are not the people that the Father pays the big attention to. Those are not where the nuclear genes flow. The Father has only two sons who are "the sons," two generations. One is Adam and one is Jesus. One, Paul tells us, was, to be sure, a living soul but the other is a life-giving spirit. One ceded us mortality. The other seeds us immortality.

So, we become the first people who actually get to choose our family. Actually, we need to choose which son of God we are from and in whom it is that we live.

Actually, we need to choose which son of God we are from and in whom it is that we live.

Christmas is the celebration of the choice, the potential of new birth in His birth. No Christian holiday draws us into notions of family as Christmas does. But if we allow it, His birth can shape us to a grace that will draw us as well as those that we love into the deeper tree. Through Him we enter His generation.

Tricia and I pray, that all of us born of our ancestor Adam find ourselves this season born once more into the birth, death and resurrection of the second Adam. From our family and from us to you,

PRAYER:

Jesus, You were born once that we can be born twice. From before the foundation of the world the Father planned it. Even as our father Adam fell and we all with him, the Father knew. You came to be one of us, not to remediate us, not merely to take us back to where we were before the fall. Jesus, you came rather to recreate us, a new species on the earth, born again, born of the Second Adam, in You, to live forever, with You, in a new heaven and a new earth.

On Christmas we just don't celebrate your birth. We celebrate the very sweep of your life from forever into forever. You were born to die and to live again and to ascend fully human and divine, securing our forevers as You move across time. We exalt and praise You our Most High God! Glorify yourself as You change this cosmos itself. You are most high God even at your lowliest.

And now a new heaven for us and your angels, and now a new earth to befit what you purpose for us. That was the manger potential that we will surely all realize. That is the manger potential that we see on Christmas. That was what lay latent in the baby born in Bethlehem. So we rejoice with the rest of heaven, because You came for us the first time. And You are coming for us again. Maranatha.

Letter Seventeen

2014: A VESSEL OF GOD THAT BEGETS THE VESSEL

While they were there, the days were completed for her to give birth. And she gave birth to her firstborn son; and she wrapped Him in cloths, and laid Him in a manger, because there was no room for them in the inn. Luke 2:7-8 NASB

WE CAN MISS the importance of it. But the coming of any life requires timing that intensifies itself. Sprouted blossoms require the coming of a moment. Jesus' journey from the Spirit's breath of conception to His own first breath was a nine-month fixed one. Mary was conscious of the time. The time of all times was finally near. The completion of her time harbored the completion of all time. She was pregnant with everyone's forevers and she knew it. It was prophesied by God over her ancient grandmother Eve in the garden—this seed, this coming. It was the voiced expectation of the Hebrew Prophets and the Law. Her belly held hope to those who never knew hope.

And in the end the timing of this coming hope was reduced to the tempo of a mother's pain—the focus of an adolescent heart upon the undulations of her womb. Synchronized spasms withstood in a strange place! Her mother not near! Alone but for the tic tock of a pacing Joseph! The tiny head slightly bloodied for the first time lodged at the end of the birth canal—her womb a place between two kingdoms. A crescendo of hurt and hope, and then that final push! A new One slipped from between her legs to where we are. A new holiness and a new time arrived on our earth.

And I wonder. Before she swaddled Him tight in His wrappings, as she held Him naked in her hands, half her, half Him, did she stare deep into half opened, steel blue, newborn eyes? Did she wipe away the remaining traces of crimson? Did she say to Him and to herself? "This is my body. This is my blood."

Every pregnancy is an advent and an intensifying one at that. Mary's identity as God's vessel drove the intensity of that first advent. What drives the intensity of our advent? Is it the ever-increasing demands of the "Christmas culture"- the tyranny of time, gifts, planning, money, debt and food? Or is it a time to ask ourselves, as Mary did, what child do we really carry?

What drives the intensity of our advent?

Trish and I and our family wish you all a blessed holiday season. But we also wish you a time in which you can carry life. May you bear Jesus to so many who, especially at this season, are in need of a Christ in their lives.

PRAYER:

So once again time is pregnant with your coming Jesus. The moment that Mary bore You, your time had come. Both time and your church together are pregnant again with your coming. Even as Mary gladly yielded, prepared, concentrated, and took care for your coming . . . grant your church the sense of gravitas to prepare as well. The swelling of Mary's womb was an organic clock portending the salvation of the world arrived. And the perseverance and the burgeoning of your church is a clock portending your arrival once more.

Make your body on the earth as sensitive as her body to the inevitable moment. When You were conceived and born, You were an omen to hell that its destruction was sure. And You are a sign to heaven that our forever is secured. We know Jesus that when You arrive again it will be as if all of history had been incredibly quick in the light of what awaits us. Keep us aware Jesus that the day of your arrival is as immanent as the manger day was. We expectantly pray this in your name Jesus. Amen!

Letter Eighteen

2015 GREATER THAN THE LAW

"But when the fullness of time came, God sent forth His only son, born of a woman, born under law, so that He might redeem those who were under law that we might receive adoption as sons." Galatians *4:4-5 NASB*

THIS IS Paul's Christmas picture. There is, he declares, a divine timetable—the moment when our space time universe is just poised to be breeched. The Father's cosmos ripens and the Holy Spirit acts. But how is time full and for whom?

When the time arrived to conceive, Mary never actually consented to Gabriel any more than a canvass consents to the artist's stroke. It was merely time for the God's splendor to descend. That was the nature of the overshadowing of her by the Spirit.

In her womb, timelessness touched time and a new time was set.

In her womb, timelessness touched time and a new time was set. And at the manger, the moment in which Mary's womb was emptied, time was full. The pregnancy of the mother ended and the pregnancy of the only Son began. This Son's life was now expectant carrying a new age replete with all of our adoptions as sons. Her blood spilled in childbirth so that His blood would be spilled for our new birth. The first Christmas peered across time to Calvary. And time mingled into already and not yet.

A Son was born under law. The fullness of time had come for law itself. No doubt, law refers to Jesus' birth under Jewish law. But Paul quite pointedly leaves out that "the." It is just naked old enslaving law that Paul cites. We are "under law." Law is more than mere religious law. Law involves all of the duties we perform that convince us that we can save ourselves. There is no end of behaviors we contrive to tell ourselves that we are in control . . . that we can be our saviors. The lie of law leads to the vanity that we can improve on God's timeless grace.

There is no end of behaviors we contrive to tell ourselves that we are in control . . . that we can be our saviors.

Herein is Christmas irony. All power in heaven and earth lays seemingly powerless in the infant boy, while we, who actually are powerless, deceive ourselves into thinking we have power to redeem our lives. And a tiny Son is greater than law. Jesus, the preexistent Son became the existent Son to relieve us of all our silly attempts to save. The infant was perfectly qualified because He too, like us, was born under law . . . and the arrow of time.

Time becomes full when God fills it. May God grant to each of us this season the Christmas realization that our time is in fact full. With that in mind, may our joy rewind the clocks of others as well. May we lean away from the sufficiency of ourselves and really declare the sufficiency of God's infinite grace. Simply put, may we help others find Jesus just in time.

Tricia and I, along with our family wish all a Merry Christmas!

PRAYER:

Save us, God, from our ever-present delusion that law is the tool we can use to save ourselves. Remind us by grace again and again that there will never be enough work, enough behavior, enough determination, enough strength, enough talent, enough prayer that we can perform to assure ourselves of our salvation. There will never be enough effort to merit us a loving relationship with You. Is that why You entered time in the image of powerlessness? Is that why an unborn child and then a born one as frail as any being could be was essential to do the redemption trick?

Lord, we know the reason that we will never accomplish your full intentions toward us. It is because the world cannot contain all of your love toward us now. We can never out love You Jesus. It is why we need forever. So by the very definition of our creation we are under achievers. Only You could achieve what the Father intended for us from the first . . . your death . . . your resurrection . . . our resurrections.

This holiday season Lord cause us to remain in awe that a child, wrapped in swaddling clothes and lying in a manger is the genesis of God's greatest achievement in the history He Himself created . . . past, present, future, forever. Amen.

mend our poverty, would You give us the gift of love to create new relationships where old ones have decayed? Would You create healing balm for so many who are suffering . . . physically . . . spiritually . . . emotionally?

Mary said, "Be it unto me." We ask in humility God, 'Be it unto them', to those who are desperate to see the creative power of your love, the force of Christmas Light. Let us take an object lesson from a young girl visited by an angel. This season we long to see the limitations of our reason defied in the greatness of your regard for us. Make something from nothing again and again. We thank You living God. Amen.

Letter Twenty

2017: SOMETHING FROM NOTHING

"God, who gives life to the dead and calls into being that which does not exist." *Romans 4: 17 NASB*

" And Mary said, "Behold, I am the servant of the Lord; let it be to me according to your word." *Luke 1:38 ESV*

THE MAGIC of prayer is to commune while creating. Prayer gathers its loftiest moment at the first Christmas. This God calls upon nothing . . . and it becomes something! In the beginning, Genesis says, God spoke a word and it was. And throughout history He speaks and it is. Every time a baby is conceived God calls into being that which does not exist. And that is just we normal babies!

But Christmas is the supreme iteration of what God calls. And a Word from God fuses with the "yes" from a young virgin in Nazareth. One utterance from the virgin Mary, "be it unto me" and something which did not exist springs into being one of us . . . a whole new species of Adam. This Jesus!

The shadow power of the Holy Spirit conceived Jesus in the warmth and the wet of Mary's womb. All the God-ness of the Son that forms and informs all creation, that drives all creation, came to rest in a tiny one. There was no sonogram to hear, no doctor to see. Only the ear of Joseph upon Mary's belly all those months, getting wind of the heartbeat of the sustainer of worlds. The Word became flesh to dwell among us.

Herein lies the prayer puzzle of Christmas. Was Mary's role as trifling as we pretend? Was the Holy Spirit simply seeking some surrogate womb to harbor the little Word. Was Mary's agency in this creation merely to ally herself to God?

It is deeper. It always is when the word of God creates through us. Mary's word "be it unto me" is not mere acquiescence to Gabriel or God. Her yes is communion. High intimacy with God who calls into being! When we say "yes" to God's personal purpose for us, it is union and intimacy. That is the deepest prayer. As God calls into being the things that we yearn for, we have the privilege of communing with Him over His word.

As God calls into being the things that we yearn for, we have the privilege of communing with Him over His word.

So . . . what are the nothings in our lives this Christmas that need to become somethings? Where is the void that we carry with us that we yearn for God to fill with a word from heaven? He calls into being that which does not exist. And Christmas is all about a word . . . of prayer. A Word from God became Word within Mary. And the Word became flesh and dwelt among us.

This is the prayer of Trish and me and our family. Let all of the nothings that we face in our lives, the chasms and emptiness that long to be filled, let them become communions with the Father that, in turn, "yes" each of us into our destinies.

PRAYER:

Jesus, our prayers mingled with intimacy with You create the capacity to make something of nothing. We confess that there are voids in our lives which become especially apparent during this season. As we voice our prayers before You, would You send your Holy Spirit to create somethings from all of the human nothings that beset us? In your goodness would You create resources to mend our poverty, would You give us the gift of love to create new relationships where old ones have decayed? Would You create healing balm for so many who are suffering . . . physically . . . spiritually . . . emotionally?

Mary said, "Be it unto me." We ask in humility God, 'Be it unto them', to those who are desperate to see the creative power of your love, the force of Christmas Light. Let us take an object lesson from a young girl visited by an angel. This season we long to see the limitations of our reason defied in the greatness of your regard for us. Make something from nothing again and again. We thank You living God. Amen.

Letter Twenty-One

2018 CHANGE OF AGE

". . . Elizabeth was barren . . . advanced in years . . . After these days Elizabeth his wife became pregnant, and she kept herself in seclusion for five months . . . . Now in the sixth month the angel Gabriel was sent from God to a city in Galilee called Nazareth to a virgin. . .Behold your cousin Elizabeth . . . in her sixth month." Luke 1:7, 24, 26, 36 NASB

THE FULLNESS of time on that first Christmas is not marked by a pendulum. . . nor the specificity of an atomic clock. The first Christmas Calendar tics and tocs to the flow of gestations. Two wombs timely matched, two covenants, two ages, synchronized one in hope realized and the other hope surprised. Luke sees to it that we recognize God's tempo. Gabriel's arriving with His proposal to Mary is pegged to Elizabeth's prenatal holiness in the womb John the Baptist calls home.

All of the years of Elizabeth's disappointment, the exhausted, seemingly fruitless years until her menopausal clock stopped! And in that culture her marked barrenness was failure. Elizabeth never knew! Her womb was destined to be the time keeper for the changer of ages. And as Mary and Elizabeth for three months hugged and touched tummies, the one who culminated the ending age was filled with the Holy Spirit. And the Incarnate one who initiates the new age . . . well . . . His heart was beginning to beat.

In impatience, frustration, disappointment or even anger, how do we reckon our own time? What is our reference? We rarely know in advance how the timing of God for our lives is enmeshed in the purpose of God for the lives of others. Time telling in the Kingdom of God calibrates to heaven's purposes far beyond our designs. When we live where we live, for how long we live, like Elizabeth and Mary, our clocks are wound by the one we live for.

Trish and I pray that in this particular Christmas season we all keep time with that spirit of the first Christmas. May the power of the Holy Spirit set the sense of what unique season it is for each of us, synchronize our lives to the importance of our living for all of those others to whom we are called.

Prayer:

Oh Father! You are the Creator, Keeper of the times and seasons of our lives. Your word says that You ordain the places that we dwell and the very times that we dwell there. The times we observe are created by the movement of the cosmos that You set into motion-the sun moon and stars. We know that the meaning of our times and seasons are set to your purposes in a lost world who needs You. The cosmos moves to address the destitute and lowly of heart.

So even as Mary sought Elizabeth at the right time for each of them, synchronize our lives with those who need You. Let us become timekeepers of hope for the hopeless. Let us be living confirmation to others, like Elizabeth was to Mary, that the deepest hope that they dare to hope will be realized because You are our good Father.

Every Christmas is new Lord. We long to touch others that they can be blessed and realize that God has a design and a means to accomplish what is in store just for them. We ask for divine appointments . . . fill the cosmic calendar . . . so that like Mary and Elizabeth we can be living visitations as well. Amen.

Letter Twenty-Two

2019 EXECUTORS OF PROTECTION

". . . for Herod is going to search for the Child to destroy Him." So Joseph got up and took the Child and His mother while it was still night, and left for Egypt." Matthew 2:13-14 NASB

RESIDENT in our cultural Christmas pieces are angels and shepherds and wise men and Glories to God and the steel assurance of fulfilled prophecy. However, on the first Christmas, Mary had a little lamb and it was in peril. Lurking peril lies at every frayed edge of Christmas. The living Madonna and child in the sites of homicidal madmen! Really? The Holy refugees ushered off to a continent where yet today the majority of refugees are marooned?

But the greatest menace of the matter is the certainty that Herod and his assassins are no accident. Here lies the unclearness of God incarnate. Why would God call into being the Christ child, destined to die for us all, to redeem us all, then lay the baby in jeopardy of being a holy victim thirty years before His time.

The baby Jesus is vulnerable and mortal in the angel's challenge to Joseph a life time before Jesus' immortality was to be proven.

"Arise!" That is what the angel said. Arise hero Father of the first Christmas! Extract the mother and child from the nerve center of a world's lust for power. And Joseph's embrace of human fatherhood makes him the deliverer of Joseph's own deliverance. Joseph is the savior of his Savior and the protector of his Protection. He secures the One who is his own security. So why then does the promise of God need protection?

So why then does the promise of God need protection?

The answer is woven into the reality of the humanity of God. We are frail and vulnerable. The presence of the power of God doesn't absolutely insulate us from the peril of the cruelty of Satan and the consequences of sin. The sinless One was born to share in our peril. In order to be us He must be frail and vulnerable as well. Otherwise His coming to be us would be a pretense of humanity. And the irony is that in His frailty we are able to see ourselves, and we become vessels of protection to whatever He calls into being.

Our enemy hunts down what God calls into being. And then God makes us executors of protection so that His purpose is accomplished on the earth.

Trish and I pray during this holiday season that any promise from God you have received would be especially protected. May you have attendant angels as well. May faith like Joseph's and Mary's cause you to steward faithfully what He is speaking into being through you to have faith for.

PRAYER:
Lord God, we ask You to forgive us a most persistent

complaint . . . we grumble to heaven that your promises constantly seem to arrive in the midst of peril. Nothing is easy we lament.

Yet your very birth, Jesus, was beset by the enemy who sought to destroy You. And You and those given to protect You needed to move in deep discernment and faith to see You protected and the scriptures fulfilled.

Forgive us the trespass of thinking that your Kingdom comes without vulnerability, struggle or, at times, violence, cruelty and the assaults of hell. Your whole mission to be incarnate was to empathize perfectly with us, for You yourself to be a perfection for us to live up to. We know this culminated in your sacrificial crucifixion for us. But the genesis was in the plan of your birth before Genesis itself.

Forgive us for frustrated utterances which say that following You is inconvenient, sacrificial and trying. Grace us to understand that although the first Christmas was centered on a powerless One, its resolution was the manifestation of the All Powerful. Manifest yourself in us through humility, faith, love and strength. . . manifest in all of us who, through Advent, populate the story of your nativity. Amen.

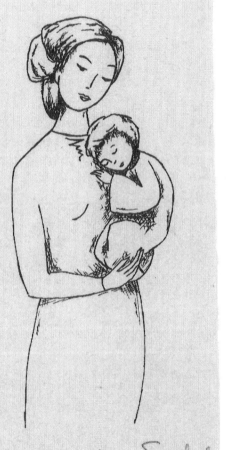

21/100 Christmas '75   Steckel

Letter Twenty-Three

2020 CHOSEN TO LOVE

"And His mercy is upon generation after generation. Toward those who fear Him." Psalm 103:17 NKJV

"He has done mighty deeds with His arm; He has scattered those who were proud in the thoughts of their heart. He has brought down rulers from their thrones, And has exalted those who were humble. He has filled the hungry with good things; And sent away the rich empty-handed." Luke 1:50-53 NASB

THE LYRICS ARE MARY'S. The later titled song is *Magnificat*. The occasion is confirmation. Elizabeth's greeting and blessing confirm that all Gabriel declared to Mary is true . . . is God. We don't honor Mary for some native innocence nor for some supposed naiveté. Mary was a feisty young lady full of an agility with the scripture and full of the right kind of fear. As Elizabeth blessed her she explodes into a praise laden theology and understanding beyond the supposed reach of simple Hebrew girls. Or so we would think. Mary's song models a meekness not mild and a humility unrestrained.

And this is what she declares. That mercy of the Lord has great reach. It reaches as far as the fear of God goes. Mary's womb is chock full of God's mercy toward generations, mercy toward the generations that preceded her, mercy from Adam to Adam, and mercy toward the generations that would follow her, from second Adam to the Second Coming of the second Adam. So if we want to see God's mercy, well, follow the fear of Him.

Mary gets to be, then, the show-and-tell of what she sings and celebrates. She is the counter intuitive mother of ultimate royalty. Jesus' mom's heart carries no personal pride in how she is blessed. She is bereft of wealth and comfortable with no significant status on earth. Her fear of being misunderstood and vilified as out-of-wedlock is suffused in her fear of being unwilling to love the Father in the way the Father has chosen for her to love Him, to bear His only begotten Son.

Let's ask ourselves a question. During this Christmas season what way has God chosen for us to love him? Trish and I wish that love would carry us as far as the fear of God goes. For that is the place where mercy lives. So we can bear Jesus to some who are lost. We wish the same, this season, for you.

PRAYER:

Lord forgive us for all those persons and things that we fear far above our fear of You. You know the truth God. You know us. You know that we fear people. We fear circumstances. We fear possibilities, we fear dangers which possibly even should be feared. But when we fear them above the fear of You they become our idols.

This Christmas, Lord Jesus, let us let loose our idols and follow the exemplar of your mother. She feared not following your Spirit wherever He leads more than she feared for her reputation, feared a maniacal king, a misunderstanding husband, all of the enmity that hell could muster.

The purveyors of news trade in the commodity of fear. When the media sets us awash with worldly fears, we ask, Holy Spirit, that You create a supernatural standard. We ask that even as at the first Christmas, You reveal a prince of peace. He came so all of us would fear You God. Let them know His name is Jesus, begotten not made, who for us came down from heaven that we would be free from the destruction of fear in our lives. Hosanna!

Letter Twenty-Four

2021 STARSHINE

---

*"Where is He who has been born King of the Jews? For we
saw His star in the east and have come to worship Him . . .
they went their way; and the star, which they had seen in the
east, went on before them until it came and stood over the
place where the Child was. When they saw the star, they
rejoiced exceedingly with great joy." Matthew 2:2, 9-10*

STARSHINE IS special to people in different ways. Most of us
merely enjoy the aesthetic awe of having these stars, lights in our
sky to charm our nights, to render us poetry, myth, songs and
romance. That is one wonder of starlight. Then there are those of
us a little more familiar with the night's lights, they move and
direct us. They tell sailors up from down and there from here. We
live by their predictability. But scientific gazers find wonder in the
consciousness that each light is the signal of some older reality.
Each point of light is a created sun somewhere spewing waves of
light across millennia to be probed and measured.

Magi were night-sky hybrids--part astronomer part astrologer.
We are in awe at the astronomer part, these forerunners of true

JACK GROBLEWSKI

scientists. But the astrologer part, not so much. Astrology being superstition and all! And yet it wasn't the stellar theorems that made the wise men wise. It was their ability to find meaning in the light. The light wasn't merely a light of direction. It first had to be a light of revelation. And it was the revelation that charmed them. Astronomers look up and see space. Magi look up and see heavens.

When the new light appeared, whether comet or supernova or angel, it was laden with meaning. Truth seeded what the astrologer saw and launched them on a journey. They chased a truth the astronomers today would have missed. After all, the keepers of the sacred Book missed it. Kings and scholars never caught wind that it was time for a chase. When we chase what we know in order to honor it, God isn't concerned with our pedigree as much as with our hearts.

This season Trish and I pray that the God of Christmas starshine still cause us to chase His light. May He not enlighten the eyes of our minds more than the eyes of our hearts. We pray that what our hearts are given to see will be more than what our minds merely see. We pray light will carry us to the place where the only option is to rejoice, to kneel, and simply adore Jesus.

PRAYER:

Something there is in us that seeks an illumination. Father God, we know that it wasn't the star itself that set the Magi on their journey. It was the revelation that the star engendered. Before the birth of the Messiah, the Holy Spirit birthed in Gentiles a curiosity and then a light in the heavens. The star was the first Christmas gift. It set them on a quest to give gifts themselves.

Lord, as a Christmas gift to us, would You birth in each of us anew a holy curiosity, one that sets us on a journey to deepen our discovery of You. Our passion is that this coming year You would direct the curiosity that You created in us toward You in some

94

way. Whether it be exploring a facet of your creation or whether it be a percolating of the creativity You created in us. We ask for an illumination . . . and a journey. And as we follow, Jesus, we ourselves will lay our treasures at your feet. . . and adore You. Amen.

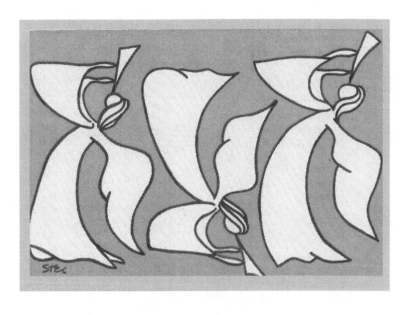

Letter Twenty-Five

2022 SALVATION'S NAME

"And at the end of eight days, when he was circumcised, he was called Jesus, the name given by the angel before he was conceived in the womb." Luke 2:21 ESV

HERE IS a forgotten end piece of most of our Christmases . . . the first time the Son of God spilled blood. His circumcision! His now new name, Jesus, means "salvation." Here is Salvation's blood flowing as He comes under the dictates of the Law. His same spilled blood would relieve us of the curse of that Law thirty years later. His rent baby flesh, our High Priest's foreskin falls as covenant is cut by the low priest. A little first-time victim no doubt squalling that day. This same flesh broken is to be pierced on Calvary. And our end piece of Christmas is the beginning piece of Easter.

Doesn't the pretty part of Christmas pass quickly? This is the bookend of Incarnation. And it is all about identity and humility. When Jesus' ancestor Abram was circumcised he received a name, Abraham, and a greater identity. In submitting to the requirement of the law He came to fulfill, Jesus receives a name and a people. Jesus is now legally Joseph's child. The tribe of Judah has a son and a king. God one of us is God with us!

His now new name, Jesus, means "salvation."

But the grand irony is that, unlike us, the Sinless One neither needs His flesh nor His heart circumcised. His purpose is to be like us. His identity is in His identification with us, our powerlessness and the spectrum of our poverty.

For many who celebrate Christmas, the celebration of Jesus' circumcision comes those eight days after the presents are unwrapped. For all of the world's intents and purposes, the party is over. Most people hardly reflect on these remains of the first Christmas. Our tinsel is frayed. And the holiday is tired. We face the new year full on. Yet this is where the lesson of this year's Christmas begins to be displayed.

This year Tricia and I pray for all of us. As the made up magic becomes stripped away by life's grit, this is when the circumcised one named Jesus is most with us. For this new year may all the Christmas presents be supplanted by His circumcised presence for all the days of the year. Through each speed bump or trial may we all deeply sense His constant identification. Jesus with us.

PRAYER:

Jesus, our Circumcised One. Even your first blood was spilled on our behalf. From your conception to your ascension, it is all a manifestation of your humility. Even as a newborn You never saw equality with God as something to be clung to. But You, in perfect innocence, submitted yourself to the very law that You would fulfill and complete. You did it just to be completely identified with us and our struggle with sin and its consequences.

God, so much of the celebration of your birth has come to involve grasping at things...who gets the best gifts, who offers the most opulent festivity, which church's Christmas pageant is the finest, all the crazy striving for Christmas to be perfect. We mistreat our families with exasperating holiday expectations. All this Lord, when the perfection of Christmas is actually a model of perfect humility. Jesus help us, through this season to humble ourselves, help us to see your coming as an embodiment of both humanity and divinity but also of humility. Ahhh, the loveliness of your Godly emptiness!

At the manger, Jesus, we realize finally that humility itself is an attribute of God. Grant that we can somehow actually see it. Grant that we likewise can be Godly and empty and live that out in all that we celebrate. Amen. And Merry Christmas.

MORAVIAN STAR

The Moravian star is a symbol of the birth of
Jesus and the star of Bethlehem. The star is
often made of paper and is illuminated so it
shines from within. The points of the star
radiating out from the center represent
Jesus' universal love and concern for all of
mankind. The star is hung the first Sunday of
Advent and remains up until Epiphany,
January 6. The Moravian Church adopted the
star as a symbol of Christ's birth and
incorporated it into Advent and Christmas
displays. The star has become a popular 1st
Advent craft tradition in many families.

Incarnate

"The central miracle asserted by Christians is the Incarnation.
They say that God became Man. Every other miracle prepares for
this, or exhibits this, or results from this."
- C.S. Lewis, *Miracles*

Deum de Deo, lumen de lúmine, Deum verum de Deo vero,
génitum, non factum, consubstantiálem Patri:
per quem ómnia facta sunt.

God from God, light from light, True God from True God,
Begotten not made, one in being with the Father,
Through whom all things were made.
- *Nicene Creed*

ADVENT IN MANY CHRISTIAN CHURCHES is the season of
preparation for the celebration of the birth of Christ. Since Jesus'
birth has historically happened, there can be an irony about
calling the church to prepare for it. In other words, what is vital
about spiritual preparation for an event that has already occurred?
To give Advent a deeper relevance, the Church has historically
conflated Jesus' first coming with His second coming, the latter,

of course, having not yet occurred. But despite that liturgical aim, Advent today for most Christians remains focused on the nativity events. Practically speaking it is all about Christmas; that is, Jesus' conception, incarnation and birth.

Formally, Advent is a religious season with no claims to secular celebration. But in effect, given the marketers and myth-makers and various forms of media in the past century, and given the fact that in America it is sandwiched between Thanksgiving and Christmas, Advent is unwittingly but differently celebrated in the secular arena as well. The word "Advent" would never be used, but the commercial arena certainly prepares heavily for the arrival of Christmas. Marketers of all faiths surely find the weeks leading up to Christmas highly advantageous (or shall we say, "advent"—ageous!) to their bottom lines.

So, we have Christmas stories, and productions and tinsel and lights and froth. And I harbor no jealousy that the season has been co-opted by the world, but it does lead to a notion in the church that the warmth and festivity generated during the season is, in fact, all there is to Advent.

There is a doctrine underlying Christmas, and it is foundational to everything that Christianity stands upon. The name of that doctrine is Incarnation...

But because of all this, it needs to be said: There is a doctrine underlying Christmas, and it is foundational to everything that Christianity stands upon. The name of that doctrine is Incarnation, the mystery through which God become man and yet remains both God and man! The intention of this section, the third portion of this Advent-themed book, is to encounter and consider the Incarnation of Jesus whereby He became fully God and fully man. I use words like "encounter" and "consider," because the goal is less a theological understanding and more an interaction with the enormity of the mystery. My hope is that we can mine the depth of this truth in a more conversational rather than scholarly way.

After all, it was primarily this mystery, the Incarnation of Christ, that occupied the church at large for its first three hundred years. The Apostle's Creed, the earliest and most concise declarative prayer of the early church, states in profundity veiled only by its directness, that Jesus was "conceived by the Holy Spirit and born of the virgin Mary." But the succinct simplicity of those words proves to be enough to ignite three hundred years of theological tussles and church counsels across the known world to deal with the enormity of what that means for we who believe. The church was attempting to discern and understand more specifically how this vital mystery should inform and affect the way we pray and worship.

As a result, the term "Incarnation" has been defined theologically, that is, as much as one can "define" a mystery. And still, the unique divinity of the man, Jesus of Nazareth, remains much the stumbling block for a world loathe to give credence to such a supernatural notion--especially if any acceptance of it involves a single ounce of moral obligation.

Several years ago, I watched an interview with Bono, the lyricist and songwriter from the group U2, in which he was queried regarding his faith. While the interviewer wasn't hostile, it seemed that he was attempting to incite Bono to somehow limit the Godhood of Jesus. He seemed mildly irritated with Bono's answers and continued pressing harder with this theme of questioning. And we find splayed across the ages this same arrogance of intellectuality manifested as a real gut disdain for the idea of God become one of us.

I have come to this conclusion: it is in the interest of our carnality to make of Jesus something less than He is. Because if we can do that, then the moral choices that our belief in Him requires becomes manageable. What a Jesus who is merely human asks of us can be mitigated or even ignored. If Jesus is another philosopher or teacher with a wonderful idea, how much less will we need to face what the cross and the resurrection mean in terms of the ways that we conduct our lives—never mind dealing with realities beyond, such as new heavens and new earths!

Paul, the Apostle born out of due season, wows us with his climbs of comprehension of the Incarnate One as he unfolds it in his epistle to the Philippians and Colossians. And before that, the Apostle John lets us into his perception of Incarnation, an almost esoteric mystery of an Incarnate Word showing an acute awareness of Jesus' pre-existence. His is the fourth and last gospel and he chooses to begin with the mystery.

But the actual moments in time and space inaugurating the Incarnation are two unique occurrences: conception and birth! Luke recounts both and is the only one who does. Notably Luke, usually a stickler for detail, gives himself to understatement in both cases. Here his gospel describes Mary at the very moment when the Christ child was conceived:

And Mary said to the angel, "How will this be, since I am a virgin?" And the angel answered her, "The Holy Spirit will come upon you, and the power of the Most High will overshadow you; therefore the child to be born will be called holy—the Son of God. And behold, your relative Elizabeth in her old age has also conceived a son, and this is the sixth month with her who was called barren. For nothing will be impossible with God." And Mary said, "Behold, I am the servant of the Lord; let it be to me according to your word." And the angel departed from her. Luke 1:35-38 ESV

Compacted into this brief exchange between angel and adolescent is all the substance of the Incarnation. Virgin birth! God and man! Messiah! Word made flesh! No wonder the angel adds, "Nothing will be impossible with God."

In the Greek text, Mary utters only six simple words in response to this news from Gabriel, and in the Aramaic language, which they would have been speaking, it is even less. Yet these few words change the course of history. When Mary declares, "Let it be to me according to your word," the cosmos itself is altered. "Unto me" is the momentous moment when biologically and supernaturally, creation and Creator align and become one. The chemistry of mundane creation is interrupted and superseded. The near brusqueness with which Gabriel departs underscores that his mission culminated at the very point of her submission.

Jesus was conceived differently from any other human being ever conceived, but he wasn't different simply because he was both God and man. He was different because He was a new kind of man, a man who could reproduce himself in a new kind of way that would not be sexual but rather spiritual! However, this spiritual reproduction was going to be so much more profound and real than the physical version.

Years later, when Paul needs to enlighten the Corinthian church regarding the essential truth of Jesus' conception and birth, he also emphasizes the new species upon the earth that Jesus has pioneered. His words help form the foundation of our understanding of the new creation and, in turn, our own future resurrections. Paul describes it in these two passages in his letter:

""For as by a man came death, by a man has come also the resurrection of the dead. For as in Adam all die, so also in Christ shall all be made alive." 1 Cor. 15:21-23 ESV

Thus it is written, "The first man Adam became a living being"; the last Adam became a life-giving spirit. But it is not the spiritual that is first but the natural, and then the spiritual. The first man was from the earth, a man of dust; the second man is from heaven. As was the man of dust, so also are those who are of the dust, and as is the man of heaven, so also are those who are of heaven. Just as we have borne the image of the man of dust, we shall also bear the image of the man of heaven." 1 Cor. 15: 45-49 ESV

When Paul says that the second Adam became a life-giving spirit, he is not merely describing Jesus' death and resurrection, but, importantly, His conception and birth. Paul is informing us that Christmas is not just celebrating baby Jesus as another man among men called by God. Jesus is not like Moses or Elijah, nor is the baby Jesus some super form of us who resembles a religious action hero.

What is more wondrous is that this baby Jesus is not extra-human. He is not an alien from heaven, something mystical and removed. The baby Jesus is a totally new and unique creative act representing a whole new beginning for every one of us forever. Colossians 1:15 declares that He is "the firstborn of all creation." Paul is proclaiming that in Christ a new order of humanity is now arrived first in the womb of a virgin, and then in a manger in a dusty corner of the earth.

You see, God's design is grander than our individual redemptions. The first Adam chose to sin and, consequently, sin and death entered the world. The second Adam would not sin so that we could become new creations ourselves. We, in the likeness of the second Adam, will live such that we cannot sin because there will be no sin in the new heaven and earth. By biological birth we share in the life of the first Adam. But by choice, we share in the life of the child conceived and born to be the Son of God.

Luke is just as succinct in his approach to the birth event of Jesus as he is in the account of His conception. It is remarkable that in Luke's description of Mary's delivery, the very moment of Jesus' birth becomes an event that is related uneventfully! After the appearance of the angel Gabriel, the miracle of Jesus conception, the "Magnificat" salvation song of Mary, and the Holy Spirit filled visitation with Elizabeth which included prophecy and worshipping babies in utero, along comes this bare-boned statement in Luke.

"And while they were there, the time came for her to give birth. And she gave birth to her firstborn son and wrapped him in swaddling cloths and laid him in a manger, because there was no place for them in the inn." Luke 2:6, 7 ESV

With all the excitement and anticipation expressed surrounding Jesus' conception, we might easily wonder as we read about his birth, "Is that all there is?" As we consider Luke's careful detailing of history elsewhere, we need to take careful note: *that is* all there is—for a good reason. Luke is making a remarkable understatement here: The delivery and manner of birth of the baby Jesus was like the delivery and manner of the birth of any child across history. Luke is telling us this: 'The Christ-child is fully normally human as well as fully unimaginably God."

'The Christ-child is fully normally human as well as fully unimaginably God."

But, standing out in Luke's economy of writing about the birth, there is one particular aspect that is unusual. It is one sign that needs to be considered, a sign which preoccupies Luke. The sign is the fact that Jesus is laid in a manger, a feeding trough for animals, and he is swaddled. Luke states in verse 7 this popularly quoted but significantly overlooked piece of the story:

"And she gave birth to her firstborn son and wrapped him in swaddling cloths and laid him in a manger, because there was no place for them in the inn." Luke 1:7 ESV

And, as we read of the angels appearing to the shepherds tending their flocks in verses that follow, the significance of this is highlighted. "And this will be a sign for you: you will find a baby wrapped in swaddling cloths and lying in a manger."

So, the swaddling cloths and a manger become a prophetic detail that rises to the status of a sign that we should note! Verse 16 tells us again that ". . . they went away in haste and found the baby lying in a manger." The babe was not suckling at his mother's breasts or held in his father's arms. The Holy Spirit is leading us somewhere and this is the sign. Interestingly, in the very beginning of the Book of Isaiah, which contains so much Messianic prophecy, God complains as to the lack of knowledge or insight in His people concerning who He is as their God. In Isaiah 1:3 God says:

> *"The ox knows its owner,*
> *and the donkey its master's crib,*
> *but Israel does not know,*
> *my people do not understand."*

Isaiah prophesies a picture of the first Christmas! All of Judaism who were awaiting the birth of a Messiah missed it, clouded by their preoccupations: the Pharisees with all their law; the Sadducees with all their politics, the Essenes with all their mysticism and even the priests with all their sacrifices! As God says, my people do not understand. They missed the obvious because the obvious didn't fulfill their preconception of how God was going to arrive.

God's people missed the coming of a Master whose crib turned out to be a manger. Jesus, the Messiah, came among oxen and asses and shepherds and gentile astronomers. Two thousand years later, as we celebrate the birth of our Messiah, we can also miss Him, or at least miss the understanding of His coming that is the very source of our celebration. We can still miss Him in His essence as He came.

Jesus was born as we are born, through our mother's pain, through the bloody passage from womb to midwife. Elyse Fitzpatrick's study of the Incarnation, *Found in Him,* describes the process in this passage:

"Within the darkness of the virgins' womb, the eternal Word entered an ovum, and took to Himself chromosomes, blood, flesh, and bone. The Word who was made flesh gestated within her for nine months. (Luke's gospel makes the timeline clear that

Mary carried her baby to term.) God relied on a weak young teenager to sustain his life. She ate and drank and nourished this embryo (who is also the Lord of heaven and earth) from the limited resources of her own little body. In his humanity he knew the restraint of living within a uterus, completely confined in deep darkness. He felt it when his mother labored. And although he did not understand the process, like every infant before him he struggled to be free and to breathe. He was born placenta and all first blood as he came forth from the virgin's womb, a strange shrine for our God."[1]

Most of us know what is being recounted in the passage, but I'm not sure, however, that we all understand it. When we attempt to believe that Jesus is God, we image it as if Jesus' human-ness merely conceals His God-ness. We tend to see it like Clark Kent and Superman or Peter Parker and Spiderman. Jesus is God who just looks like us and pretends to be one of us. We sing the stanza from Charles Wesley's brilliant hymn "Hark the Herald Angel's Sing." And I believe we misunderstand the verse:

Veiled in flesh the Godhead see.
Hail the Incarnate Deity.
Pleased with us in flesh to dwell
Jesus our Emmanuel.

When Wesley writes "veiled in flesh," he doesn't mean that Jesus' humanity is meant to hide the fact that He is really God. He means that Jesus human-ness adorns His God-ness so that in Jesus we can see who God is. But more than that, Jesus models who we are to be.

Jesus is fully one of us, and that presents a big problem. How could God manage His own seeming reduction into a helpless child? How could God accept upon Himself things like vulnerability and limited understanding and growth? How could God need the hugs of his mother, not to mention a diaper change?

How could the living Word Himself have to learn to say His first word? How could the Logos limit himself to a body with the problems of hair and teeth and eyesight and bowels? How could He live inside a human personality and submit himself to the same dark conflicts that every one of us live with?

But that mystery is Christmas itself. Somewhere in that little head, that could have been crushed easily by one of Herod's soldier's swords, galaxies drift across the universe and electrons vibrate, and we ourselves live and move and have our being. In Paul's letter to the Colossians, Paul expresses it this way: "In Him the whole fullness of the Godhead dwells bodily." (Colossians 2:9) That statement was as difficult for Paul to take on board intellectually as it is for us.

He did this so that He would not be superman and therefore someone whose example we could never possibly follow.

The amazing thing is that when the son of God became the firstborn of Mary, He did not renounce any of His God-ness to be human. Every bit of the God-ness of Jesus is latent in the baby Jesus while not manifestly realized. He did this so that He would **not** be superman and therefore someone whose example we could never possibly follow. He never moved in the miraculous nor withstood temptation out of His God-ness, but rather modeled a life we ourselves can aspire to from our human position, aware that we are not the only begotten son of God. We can never excuse ourselves for the way we act or the way that we don't act by looking at Jesus and saying, "Yeah, well, that's Jesus. That's not us."

This suggests for us an enormous responsibility. The Incarnation and Jesus' own ministry as a human on earth generate far-reaching effects on the church and each individual believer's ministry. ***In Jesus birth, God became an indistinguishable*** *part of creation so that we bear the responsibility to distinguish Him for others!*

How are we going to do that this Christmas? How do we communicate the truth of the Incarnation of the Most High God? Do we realize how seemingly crazy what we believe seems to an unbeliever? We find an answer in one of the least recognized and understood aspects of Christian belief: The Ascension.

The goal of Jesus' Ascension was His enthronement at the right hand of the Father. In describing this upcoming Ascension, Jesus says to the surprise and dismay of His disciples, "It is to your advantage that I go away." (John 16:7) And as the disciples protest, He adds that if He ascends, the Father will send the Comforter or the Holy Spirit to empower the church.

The full scope of the doctrine of the Ascension is beyond this discussion. But what we can appreciate here, especially as it relates to the Incarnation, is the truth that even now, at the right hand of the Father, there is Jesus who remains God in the flesh—still fully human, even in body! This wondrous reality escapes many.

Years ago, the church I was pastoring sent a number of worship teams to a conference where the keynote speaker, a worship leader himself, expounded on a bodily Christ with the Father in heaven and the meaning and import of that in worship. To my bewilderment, this group of seasoned believers came home and asked me what I thought about a bodily Christ being with the Father. How could they not know, I thought, that the Incarnate One is forever incarnate? And at His future coming He will be that matured Incarnate One who began as a baby in Bethlehem!

There appears to be a murky notion regarding this in the church, as if Jesus was born and His divinity simply remained masked by flesh until it was manifest in His miraculous ministry and ultimate death and resurrection. The church often assumes that He remained manifestly Incarnate in resurrection until He ascended to the Father, where he cast off the trappings and limitations of the flesh and became fully divine again, finally reigning spiritually in heaven. But bodily . . . not so much.

The truth is this: Jesus was born fully human and sinless. He lived fully human and sinless. And He is Lord God forever, fully human and sinless. His humanity never detracted from the fullness of His deity. The same Jesus Incarnate, fully human in the womb of Mary, is at the right hand of the Father empathizing with us in our humanity and interceding for us. His humanity still does not detract from the fulness of His deity.

Where then does the doctrine of Incarnation come home to roost for us as believers on a day-to-day basis? How is it "our daily bread"? The "hidden-ness" of Jesus' divinity begets a responsibility for us to reveal Him to a lost world, and this is by design. There are a multitude of ways that Christ is revealed through us but three that predominate.

The first has to do with Jesus' ascension and current position as the Incarnate One at the right hand of the Father—His "leaving us" so that we can on a daily basis do the works of the Father. John's gospel takes great care to expose the motives of heaven for the ascension of Jesus as well as its interplay with the Incarnation. In one instance recorded by John, Phillip confronts Jesus, explicitly asking Him to show the disciples the Father. Jesus' response is His clearest declaration of divinity:

"Have I been with you so long, and you still do not know me, Philip? Whoever has seen me has seen the Father. How can you say, 'Show us the Father'? [10] Do you not believe that I am in the Father and the Father is in me? The words that I say to you I do not speak on my own authority, but the Father who dwells in me does his works. [11] Believe me that I am in the Father and the Father is in me, or else believe on account of the works themselves. [12] Truly, truly, I say to you, whoever believes in me will also do the works that I do; and greater works than these will he do, because I am going to the Father. [13] Whatever you ask in my name, this I will do, that the Father may be glorified in the Son. [14] If you ask me

anything in my name, I will do it." John 14:9-14 ESV (underline added)

Two important dimensions of Incarnation are highlighted by Jesus Himself in this passage. The first is Jesus' assertion that He is one with the Father. But the second, which He explicitly states, is what we often miss: The works of the Father that were initiated by the Incarnate Christ are to be continued by us because He is with the Father. And our works of the Father will be greater.

> *The works of the Father that were initiated by the Incarnate Christ are to be continued by us because He is with the Father. And our works of the Father will be greater.*

In a metaphorical sense, we become the "Incarnations" of Jesus upon the earth, not the only begotten Son of God, but still sons of God! What was hidden at the manger and the cross, we divulge to the world in how we act and how we love. It is our responsibility to take on the character of Christ and to continue His work. And, given the context here, this includes the miraculous. Whatever we ask within the character of the name of Jesus, the Father will do. This amazing reality is a much broader topic than I have just sketched, and it has come to be known in seminaries and bible schools as "Incarnational theology." It remains a deep mystery to be lived into!

The second way that we can unfold the truth of Jesus Incarnationally is the manner in which we love, not merely in the way we love a lost world, but, more tangibly and perceptibly, the manner in which we love one another as the church. Jesus' high priestly prayer at Gethsemane was, "that they may become perfectly one, so that the world may know that you sent me and loved them even as you loved me." (The argument might be made that this is historically where the church has failed most miserably.) Jesus is paralleling His oneness with the Father with the oneness that the church can demonstrate so that the world may know Him. This, of course, is a far-reaching notion often discussed, touted and attempted less than effectively.

The church seeks to do the obvious manifest works of the Father from caring for the poor to praying for the miraculous, while manifesting the Father and Son love in our love for one another has often escaped us. And perhaps this is where Christmas and Incarnation can enter the picture more lucidly by infusing us with a theology of hope. Through intimacy with Jesus in tandem with devotion to the Advent truth and message, we can filter the ways in which we hope and what we hope in. We can imitate in our lives the God who was conceived and birthed as one of us and then died for us.

By God's grace at Christmas, we can absorb the wonder and the magic of the fact that the child in the manger was fully the God of the universe, come as an innocent infant. And somehow within the being of the baby at Mary's breast, everything that exists, from galaxies to atoms, were and are being held together. The baby's breath was the breadth of the universe's history unfolding. We can realize a bit of that without being able to rationalize it, but it becomes more ponderous when we take it to the cross.

Comprehending that a man on a cross, beaten bloody, barely breathing, tortured and trembling is fully the second person of the Trinity seems to be yet another story! We identify crucifixion as a man who is the son of God sacrificing Himself, but we don't comprehend that all of the grandeur of the Godhead was alive and well in the being that was gouged with thorns, flogged and nailed.

How could He who refused to assert Himself to escape his physical torture, be at the same time in His very being responsible for the cosmos? Every time Jesus crucified quivered uncontrollably, somewhere in His being quarks and quasars were still working the fabric of the universe simultaneously. As He was dying, He was maintaining the very lives and beings of those who were at work crucifying Him. Jesus knew it. But do we know it? Only in a perception of the enormity of the truth of the Incarnate One can the truth of the Crucifixion become realized.

> *Only in a perception of the enormity of the truth of the Incarnate One can the truth of the Crucifixion become realized.*

I honestly don't know how to do this. But I do know that Paul was determined to display this very principle in his letter to the Colossians.

> *"He has delivered us from the domain of darkness and transferred us to the kingdom of his beloved Son, ¹⁴ in whom we have redemption, the forgiveness of sins."* Col. 1:13 ESV

But who is this man who existentially accomplished this? What is the thorough nature of that person that was needed to consummate humanity's redemption and destiny? Who is this Jesus that was conceived, born and crucified? Note Paul's encompassing use of the word "all" in Colossians.

> *"He is the image of the invisible God, the firstborn of all creation. ¹⁶For by him all things were created, in heaven and on earth, visible and invisible, whether thrones or dominions or rulers or authorities —all things were created through him and for him. ¹⁷And he is before all things, and in him all things hold together. ¹⁸And he is the head of the body, the church. He is the beginning, the firstborn from the dead, that in everything he might be preeminent. ¹⁹For in him all the fullness of God was pleased to dwell, ²⁰and through him to reconcile to himself all things, whether on earth or in heaven, making peace by the blood of his cross." Colossians 1:15-20 ESV (underline added)*

While Luke's manger story uses restraint and simplicity to give us a God who is fully human, it is left to Paul to give us a human who is fully God! Christians, especially Evangelicals, acknowledge the way the commercial culture of Christmas obscures, even for the church, the true meaning of Christmas. We often are lost in the frenetic pace and pomp of the season by the time we walk into our Christmas worship. So, the question becomes: how do we react to the manger, to the truth of it all? What is to be our response?

The predominating virtue enshrined in the manger scene for humanity is hope! Jesus' existence as one of us is the product of love. But the truth of the Christ child's full identity lays latent, yet to be actualized. In fact, it is faith that will actualize all of who He is, from conception to birth to redemption to His coming again. But from the perspective of the worshipper considering the manger, hope is the conspicuous virtue. What then is hope? Hope is the positioning of my trust in something that stabilizes me so that I can cross the gap, by faith, from my present condition to the future that I live toward.

> *Hope is the positioning of my trust in something that stabilizes me so that I can cross the gap, by faith, from my present condition to the future that I live toward.*

The child in the manger was and is the stabilizing hope of heaven and earth as well as the terror of hell. He was the hope of Magi and shepherds and angels. One of the reasons that the truth of Christmas needs an advent is so that people can lay hold of the hope that is Christmas.

Life is life—filled with trials and challenges that engage our souls, our personalities, and our emotions and assault our identities as sons and daughters of God. And it can make us feel quite unstable. To the one who has children anticipating a magical

Christmas and has no job, the holidays can seem like a roller coaster. If Christmas is a time when memories of pain and dysfunction predominate, how can I be stable and anchored for those who are looking to me to provide their Christmas experience?

The author of the Book of Hebrews defines hope as that anchor for our souls (Hebrews 6:19) and we often find in liturgical art in older churches the visual sign of the anchor. As the metaphor implies, an anchor is the instrument whereby a ship that is adrift or storm-tossed can be made steady and stable. In some cases, an anchor is an instrument for survival. When a sailor throws an anchor, he wants to attach himself to something solid and safe on the sea floor below so that, even though the ride may be a bit rough, his ship can hold together until a future calm and a future port can be realized. When storm-tossed people enter the holidays asking, "How can I survive this Christmas," their answer lies in positioning their anchor of hope.

As we look at the nativity narratives in the scriptures, a principle becomes apparent. There were those who found hope in the birth of Christ and there were others who found threat, while the majority were oblivious. Who were those who found hope? Why are there those who celebrate the birth and those who merely tolerate it? It seems that . . .Those who experience wonder are those who appropriately position their hope.

Those who experience wonder are those who appropriately position their hope.

One of the more abused verses in the scripture comes from the Book of Proverbs 13: 12. *"Hope deferred makes the heart sick, but a longing fulfilled is a tree of life." NIV*

The application of this verse that we often make seems to have been forced through filters of disappointment: Because that which I hope for has not materialized in my life, God has made my heart sick. However, the writer isn't claiming that at all. The writer is challenging those who are sick at heart: *"Hope is our responsibility to cultivate. In other words: Don't defer hope, but rather direct it in the right place and your heart will not be sick and your longing will be fulfilled!"*

In the twenty-first century West, there are a whole array of places to mistakenly place one's hope. The Nativity narratives have something to say to us. Let's look at some of the first Christmas personage and ask ourselves where they placed their hope and how their experience might inform ours today.

Hope in the externals of Religion

Luke's opening to his gospel, ironically, does not begin with the appearance of the angel Gabriel to Mary. In a story recounted in Luke chapter 1, Luke recounts a parallel appearance of Gabriel to Zacharias, the husband of Elizabeth, Mary's cousin. But the consequences of Gabriel's interaction with Zacharias serve as a contrast to that of Mary. And this contrast speaks to us of hope.

Zacharias was a member of a subset of the Levitical priest-hood and was chosen by lottery from that group to tend to the temple at a particular time -- an honor that may have only happened once in a lifetime. Elizabeth was beyond her child-bearing years and was barren. While Zacharias was in the temple, Gabriel appeared to him and prophesied the pregnancy of Elizabeth and birth of John the Baptist, something that Zacharias and Elizabeth had presumably hoped for most of their lives.

Astonishingly, Zacharias flouts Gabriel's announcement and is struck dumb until the promised child is born, with Gabriel citing the reason as Zacharias' unbelief. We must wonder, in the light of the circumstances, what makes an old man do such a thing, especially since Gabriel's appearance is clearly supernatural and would have been intimidating? What makes an old man grumpy? What short-circuits the hope of the religious?

Perhaps (and quite probably), Zachariah had positioned his hope in the externals of his religion for so long that when the external duty was suddenly inhabited by the true substance of the supernatural, all he could summon was cynicism! Sadly, some of the most religious people can become the most cynical, with years of empty service born out of duty leaving no room inside for faith or belief. (I think of Thomas Merton's poem *Ode to a Severe Nun*.)

So, he was struck dumb, and one wonders whether it was a mercy. *Would his negative words have inadvertently aborted the child?* We do well to take this lesson to heart in our day, when during Advent, churches, schools and theatres are replete with pageants, plays and festivities, all of which require work and commitment that sometimes strips the season of its meaning and its joy. Ask any pastor! When our hope is in the externals of what we do in the manger season, the supernatural truth of the season can become quite distanced from our experience. It behooves us to examine various positioning possibilities of our hope, so that we can consciously choose its solid placement in anchoring truth!

Hope in a political system.

"In those days a decree went out from Caesar Augustus that all the world should be registered. [2]This was the first registration when Quirinius was governor of Syria. [3]And all went to be registered, each to his own town. And Joseph also went up from Galilee, from the town of Nazareth, to Judea, to the city of David, which is called Bethlehem, because he was of the house and lineage of David..." Luke 2:1-4 ESV

There are two gods presented in the first Christmas story.

One declares himself to be god and is not, and that one is named Augustus. The other is unable to declare anything because He is a newborn, and of course, that is Jesus and Jesus *is* God. Augustus' hope is placed in Rome and its empire. He is the first military dictator, and as such, he decrees the census with a goal of the collection of tax to fund protection from enemies both within and without. He needs this census to sustain the empire.

Jesus needs his mother's breast to sustain Him. Jesus lives, dies and is the resurrected. Augustus dies, probably poisoned by his own wife. The comparison still speaks today.

While I firmly believe in being politically involved, and while I also believe that God ordains civil authority, I am not naïve. Some political systems are better than others.We have in America the most enduring and effective one, but I am convinced that no political system is worthy of my ultimate hope. Whether you are in a funk or elated because of the results of an election, guard yourself. Sooner or later, you will learn the fragility and the limitation of politics.

I find it fascinating that most elections take place immediately previous to Advent.

Hope in Oneself

"Now after Jesus was born in Bethlehem of Judea in the days of
Herod the king, behold, wise men from the east came to
Jerusalem, saying, "Where is he who has been born king of the
Jews? For we saw his star when it rose and have come to worship
him." When Herod the king heard this, he was troubled, and all
Jerusalem with him..." Matthew 2:1, 2 ESV

Enter here Matthew's birth narrative. There is a grit to Matthew's gospel because he understands the dangers of power and control and therefore does not discount the dark side of Christmas.

People who position their hope in themselves only have room for one king in their lives: themselves!

People who position their hope in themselves only have room for one king in their lives: themselves! Placing your hope solely in yourself can doom you to becoming a narcissistic monomaniac like Herod, seeking to kill any other king that gets in your way. Or more commonly, it produces depression and disillusionment and perhaps despair.

I believe that much of the depression that rises to the fore at this time of year occurs in those who feel that their only hope is themselves and that they find themselves beyond hope. If you are reading this and count yourself as in that number and feel that isolation, let me give you another way to hope.

Hope in God and One Another

The track of this discussion is probably predictable: "Well, we don't hope in religion, politics, ourselves. It's obvious where this is going. We put our hope in God." But I want to transcend the predictable and make the argument that Mary's and Joseph's individual hope in God were each buoyed by their understanding and hope in one another. Community, and specifically the community that flows from marriage, is crucial to the outworking of hope in the Christmas story.

Mary, in her *Magnificat* salvation song before Elizabeth cries out, "All generations shall call me blessed," but that was not going to happen if Joseph decided to put her away. Her trust was in God, but there was a tacit hope in Joseph as well. Matthew 1:19

tells us that Joseph, being a righteous man and not wanting to disgrace Mary, did at first seek to put her away secretly. Joseph is characterized as deeply conflicted because the law dictated to him one thing while his heart called for another. Bypassing the turmoil of his conscious mind, an angel appears to him in a dream within the boundaries of the unconscious and there told him to do what he was disposed to do in the first place.

It is a difficult thing to hope in God without hoping in one another. We are designed for it. Christmas as well as Easter was designed for the whole community of faith, for shared worship and joy in togetherness, as well as shared response to the Incarnation and its implications in our lives.

> *Christmas as well as Easter was designed for the whole community of faith, for shared worship and joy in togetherness, as well as shared response to the Incarnation and its implications in our lives.*

But Mary and Joseph's hope in God is not the greatest hope or wonder of Christmas. There is still a greater and more amazing hope, exceeding all others! It is an unsung hope that is the essential component to Jesus' conception and birth.

God places His hope in us through Christ!

Here we revisit the enigma of Jesus' high priestly prayer asking the Father to make us one as His disciples. Any prayer prayed by Jesus it seems should encounter no hindrance, but we are forced to admit that the love He requests here has proved to be elusive! Perhaps the church has yet to grasp what Jesus was really expressing in His yearning for us to love in such a way. Jesus was not praying that we would merely be nice to one another or experience an absence of conflict. The point of Jesus' ennoblement of humankind in His incarnation was to illuminate our hearts towards the manifestation of the love that is resident in the Godhead itself. That was the hope of the living God in creating us in the first place and that is the how we glorify Him.

Martin Smith, a Christian lyricist, penned a line in one of his songs, "You have placed your hope in me." This is indeed a simple thought, but also one of the most important and sparsely recognized facets of the doctrine of incarnation. Jesus did not limit His divinity or reduce it in any way by becoming man, nor did He need to diminish humanity in any way by becoming human. In fact, it is the opposite: we became distinguished and graced among all creation! The Creator did not enter creation by becoming a galaxy or superhuman being. Rather, He became a child in a manger.

A devotional gaze into the truths of Advent, the mystery of the Incarnation and the Incarnate God Himself may just be the path forward for the church.

This is by far the greatest hope and wonder, and how often we miss it. Our Christmas lore presents the Incarnation as if the Son of God had to come "slumming" in humanity to save us. Philippians 2:6 does say that He emptied Himself, but even as He divested Himself of intrinsic power, He ennobled us! The Son of God becoming the Son of Man was not His humiliation, but rather the humility of God. He brought to the human condition a dignity and a God-likeness that changes us forever. As a result of the Incarnation, He hopes in us in Christ.

Saint Francis of Assisi designed the Franciscans' Advent devotions to focus upon and celebrate the humility of God in preparation for Christmas. I trust that those who have invested a little time in perusing these pages on Advent will encounter a sense of that humility. A devotional gaze into the truths of Advent, the mystery of the Incarnation and the Incarnate God Himself may just be the path forward for the church. It may be the journey to realizing the love and Oneness that Jesus prayed for at Gethsemane. It may be the restoration of the journey of hope.

I trust you will enjoy His coming more deeply this year as well as anticipating His sure coming again, soon.

Notes

INTRODUCTION

1. C. S. Lewis, *Screwtape Letters* (New York City, NY: HarperCollins Publishers, 2015), Chapter 8.
2. Glenn, J. (2023, January 9). *An authentic Moravian nativity scene: The Jennie Trein putz.* Glencairn Museum. https://www.glencairnmuseum.org/news letter/2019/11/19/an-authentic-moravian-nativity-scene-the-jennie-trein-putz#:~:text=The%20practice%20of%20the%20Moravian,churches%2C%20homes%2C%20and%20marketplaces.

INCARNATE

1. *Found in Him: The Joy of the Incarnation and Our Union with Christ* (Wheaton, IL: Crossway, 2013), Pg. 48.

Acknowledgments

Deepest thanks to Steve Piccione and Perrianne Brownback for editing this rather packed content and "getting me." Thanks to Kris White and Dream Tree Publishing for wisdom, layout and design. To Vince Steckle for the use of his superb artwork. And to all those who have insisted I publish these missives. Merry Christmases to come.

About the Author

Jack Groblewski pastored New Covenant Church in Bethlehem, Pennsylvania, since April of 1982. In 2022 he transitioned leadership of the church however he remains as pastor emeritus. He has a Bachelor of Arts from Kings College in Wilkes Barre, Pennsylvania and a Master's in Theology from Moravian Theological Seminary in Bethlehem, Pennsylvania. Jack is on the Executive Leadership of One Focus Network of churches, a group of churches in the US and abroad that provides support, accountability and apostolic leadership to one another. Jack is a very gifted and insightful teacher who has ministered both nationally and abroad. His teachings are mixed with humor, as well as deep theological revelations. Jack, and his wife Tricia have been married 52 years and have 4 children and 11 grandchildren. They reside in Center Valley, Pennsylvania.

Made in the USA
Middletown, DE
25 October 2023

41357584R00094